Supporting
K-5 Reading
Instruction
in the
School Library
Media Center

Lea-Ruth C. Wilkens

American Library Association
Chicago 1984

Designed by Ray Machura
Composed by Modern Typographers Inc.
in Linotron Baskerville
Printed on 50-pound Glatfelter,
a pH-neutral stock, and
bound in 10-point Carolina
cover stock by Malloy Lithographing, Inc.

Library of Congress Cataloging in Publication Data

Wilkens, Lea-Ruth C.
  Supporting K-5 reading instruction in the school
library media center.

  Includes index.
  1. School libraries—Activity programs. 2. Reading
(Primary) 3. Children—Books and reading. 4. Libraries
and education. I. Title.
Z675.S3W73 1984   027.8′222   84-460
ISBN 0-8389-0397-5

This book is dedicated to my mother and brother and to librarians who entice children into becoming lifetime readers.

Contents

Preface

This book is about how children are taught to read in the classroom and in the school library media center. Only if school library media specialists have a sound understanding of the reading instruction process will they be able to guide readers on how to use the wealth of printed materials available to them in the school library media center.

How a partnership between teacher and school library media specialist can be brought about is described for each grade level under "role of the school library media specialist." How the role of the library media specialist can be implemented is discussed in the "idea" sections. The teaching/learning suggestions provided in the "ideas," with few exceptions, are print oriented, for it is necessary to stress unequivocally that children will only learn to read when they come face to face with the printed word. Great care was taken to suggest reading ideas that can be used with children of various abilities.

The ultimate goal of this book is to convince school library media specialists that they are the professionals who can provide that special ingredient in the reading program which makes it possible for all children to read at their highest level of ability.

Reading Readiness

Why Reading Readiness?

When are children ready to learn to read? When should children be taught to read? These are two questions which have been asked by parents and educators for many years. Over the years school librarians and library media specialists probably have been asked the same questions by parents and friends who needed professional guidance in selecting appropriate reading materials for their children. Since reading readiness is of such great concern to everyone involved with teaching young children, it seemed only appropriate that a special chapter on the topic should be included in this book even though the process itself takes place before children enter school. It is hoped that the information offered on the topic will not only help school library media specialists enrich their knowledge of the entire reading process but also help them in becoming more proficient in their quest to help children become able lifetime readers.

What Is Reading Readiness?

Learning to read begins long before children enter kindergarten or first grade, with the development of reading readiness skills. These skills include auditory discrimination, visual discrimination, vocabulary development, speech development, concept development, laterality (awareness of left and right), and sequence ability. Gross and fine motor skills as well as social adjustment (getting along with peers) and emotional adjustment are also necessary for reading readiness. How each of these readiness skills may be encouraged at home, in the library, or in the child care facility will be discussed throughout the chapter.

The term "reading readiness" was first used in the 1920s, when research studies were undertaken to determine when children would be ready to read. However, throughout the years the concept of reading readiness has been somewhat controversial and even now no definition has received a widespread acceptance. Since it is beyond the scope of this book to discuss in great detail the various definitions, only several of the current viewpoints on readiness will be presented.

For example, one definition holds that reading readiness refers to that time when children are ready to begin reading print.[1] Another definition holds that a student must have a series of subskills in order to read.[2] The opposing view is, according to Fry, "that there is no point at which a child is 'ready,' but rather that reading instruction can begin at almost any age or state of development, although, of course, older or brighter children will learn faster with less repetition and effort."[3] Dolores Durkin, known for her research in early reading practices, holds that reading readiness should be examined in relation to a particular child and a particular instructional program.[4] Durkin explicitly states that this question is far more appropriate than the question, "Is the child ready?"[5] In summarizing a proposed definition of reading readiness Durkin sheds even more light on the entire concept of reading readiness:

Implicit in all these observations is that we really need to think in terms of *readiness* for reading, since some abilities will be prerequisites for one program whereas a somewhat different collection might be necessary for another one. The twofold focus also points up the folly of thinking that readiness is a uniform list of abilities that can be assessed in something like a readiness test.[6]

Psychology-based Theories of Reading Readiness

"At what age is the child ready to read?" is a question that has caused considerable debate over the years. For many years the mental age (MA) of 6.0 to 6.5, as determined by means of I.Q. tests, was accepted as standard for first grade reading readiness. The general acceptance of mental age was based on numerous research studies which were carried out in the 1920s, all of which seemed to determine that this was the appropriate age level. Durkin notes, however, that it was a 1931 report by Mabel Morphett and Carleton Washburne, which reported on the reading achievement of a group of first grade children in the Winnetka, Illinois, school, that generally established the notion that children were ready to read when they had reached the 6.0 to 6.5 mental age level.[7] Even though other studies of this time questioned the reliability of mental age as the determining factor for reading readiness, the Morphett/Washburne report overshadowed all others, and its influence was felt for many years.

During the 1950s, though, when the Russians' sent Sputnik into orbit and shook the foundations of the educational world, educators began to redirect their thoughts towards reading readiness and, instead of accepting mental age as the predominant predictor of reading success, began to consider other factors, such as environmental and maturational influences.

Proponents of the new and, one might say, enlarged view of reading readiness, were influenced by such respected educators as Jean Piaget and Jerome Bruner. Scholars who were influenced by Piaget's concepts of children's cognitive development noted that the "time common for preparation and beginning reading typically occurs just before acquisition of the concrete operational stage."[8] If reading readiness occurs before the operational stage it would then fall into what Piaget referred to as the preoperational period, which covers the ages between two and seven. However, the preoperational period was further divided by Piaget into two more specific phases. The first phase is referred to as the "preconceptual phase" and occurs between the ages of two and four years, and the second phase, the "intuitive phase," occurs between the ages of four and seven years. It is during the intuitive phase that children usually begin to indicate their readiness to read. However, it should be noted that children at this learning stage are still not able to comprehend abstract symbols, according to the theory. These children therefore need learning experiences which involve concrete objects to which labels may be attached.

Bruner's hypothesis "that any subject can be taught effectively in some intellectually honest form to any child at any stage of development,"[9] seems to contradict Piaget's hypothesis. In a sense it does, since Bruner firmly believes that children may be taught more complex subjects at an earlier age if instruction is systematic and carefully structured. Although Piaget and Bruner disagree, both dismiss the notion that there is a specific age level when children are ready to read. This concept has definitely also been reinforced through the popular television series Sesame Street, which has consistently promoted reading readiness skills to an audience of various ages. The theories have, furthermore, been evidenced in early childhood programs which have taught young children various reading readiness skills.[10]

What Readies a Child to Read?

Infants. When, how, and by whom should reading readiness be initiated? The answer is that whoever is in charge of an infant, whether this is a parent, grandparent, foster parent, or other provider of child care, is essentially responsible for taking the first steps in developing the reading readiness skills of the child. At this very early age, these skills are presented to children in an unstructured manner. Actually the development of these skills is part of the nurturing process, which depends on an intimate relationship between the child and the person in charge of the child at a particular time.

The first two skills introduced to very young children may well be *auditory discrimination* and *auditory acuity.* The natural nurturing process requires that the adults do all the talking and the infant all the listening, responding only through a bright smile, delightful babble, or crying. To develop auditory discrimination and auditory acuity in the young, parents and other nurturing adults should take every opportunity to talk to their children, whisper childlike secrets to them, and sing to them. Children who are continually involved in this one-to-one verbal interaction will not only begin to develop their auditory skills but also will be encouraged to acquire a sense and awareness of language structure itself.

Very young children may also develop *visual discrimination* when they are surrounded by visually stimulating objects and environments. Crib toys and large picture books, preferably made of cloth, help to create an awareness of colors, shapes, sizes, and broad outlines. Visual acuity and discrimination are also developed as children are introduced gradually to some of the familiar objects within the home and outside it. Trips to the supermarket, shopping mall, playground, and zoo are perfect for stimulating the child's visual alertness.

As children grow physically and mentally, the reading readiness skills should grow in their complexity. For instance, children six to eight months old can be held in one's lap and introduced to the magical and musical adventures of fingerplays and simple nursery rhymes. Very simple fingerplays in which adult and infant clap hands and touch toes using rhymes such as "Pat-a-cake," or "This little pig went to market," will help infants develop their listening skills as well as their motor skills. A couple of fingerplays can be repeated daily until the infant is quite familiar with the routines; at that point a third or fourth fingerplay may be added.

The singing or recitation of nursery rhymes such as "Rock-a-bye, baby" and "Cuckoo, cherry tree" will also help infants immeasurably in developing their auditory acuity skills. Auditory discrimination can also be helped along when a nursery rhyme such as "Polly put the kettle on," or "Little Tommy Tucker," is changed to include the infant's name.

The use of fingerplays and nursery rhymes should be continued with children nine to eighteen months old. Many children at this age level already begin take an interest in books and enjoy the experience of having an adult read familiar as well as new rhymes from a book, instead of hearing them recited from memory. It is not uncommon for children at this age level to reach for the book and make first attempts at turning pages. All of these are, of course, very important steps towards reading readiness and great care should be taken to allow the child to interact with books. At this developmental level it is also quite appropriate to take the time to point out specific objects on the page while child and adult hold the book. The adult may even wish to point a finger at certain words while reading the rhyme, giving the child opportunity to become aware that print, when read, will turn into speech. Washable, nontoxic cloth books and strong board books that do not tear easily are most practical for children at this age level.

Aside from books, children at this age level should also be given simple toys that can be pulled, pushed, stacked, or placed in some order according to size, shape, or color. By manipulating these toys children develop their motor and visual acuity skills, all of which are part of the overall reading readiness process.

Eighteen months to three years. Children have their fastest vocabulary increases between eighteen months and three years. During this period a child's vocabulary is reported to grow from about 20 words to about 1,000 words.[11] To achieve this phenomenal growth children need to be introduced to vivid, imaginative, and descriptive language. Because children develop their vocabulary on the basis of the vocabulary they hear, they should not be exposed to so-called "babytalk." Adults who interact with children of this age level must be mindful that they are the language models for the children. Children who are not spoken to or read to will have fewer opportunities to increase their vocabularies than children who enjoy active ongoing "conversations" with adults. Conversations can take place when children are fed, bathed, dressed, or played with. Certain objects should be named during these conversations and the names repeated in subsequent conversations. For example, during feeding the adult might wish to stress that the child is eating with a "spoon" and that the food itself is called "soup." Likewise, when dressing the child the adult might want to stress that the child is putting on a "blue dress" or a pair of "green pants." Through this procedure children will have many opportunities to connect the spoken word with an object. The concept of object and word can further be reinforced through books which portray in words and pictures objects familiar to the very young, such as *My First Book of Things* and *How Do I Put It On?*

Children at this age level also need the constant experience of listening to fanciful stories. Some stories, such as folktales, should be told without the use of a book so that child and storyteller can interact more closely without the interference of a book. Other stories should be read so that children can begin to perceive that words on a page can come alive through the reader. Children at this age level enjoy stories that are short and have much repetition of words and phrases; these give the children many opportunities to participate in retelling the story.

Three to five years. When children are from three to five years old, they have reached what is frequently referred to as their most "impressionable" years. It is during these years that children need to be showered with books so that they may grow steadily toward a firm desire to learn to read. They need many opportunities when they can either sit alone or with an adult and browse through books.

Books for children at this time should be as varied as children's curiosities. All children need access not only to story books, but also to books that are informational in nature and present concepts in distinct illustrative format, accompanied by precise words to capture the attention of the young "reader."

Children at this age level need to look at many alphabet books and counting books to help them develop familiarity with letter and number concepts. This is important, even now when children are exposed to letter and number concepts through television, because television images disappear within seconds, while children need to have the concepts reinforced at a more leisurely pace through books. Other readiness concepts such as awareness of laterality, opposites, and colors need to be reinforced continually through the multitudinous world of picture books.

The readiness skill of getting along with others, a prerequisite for sound learning experiences in both preschool and kindergarten, can also be furthered through books that present stories about getting along with peers. Books can also be used to help children accept themselves as worthwhile human beings and to recognize that it is all right to be different in size, shape, or skin color.

This age group definitely has not outgrown the need to listen to nursery rhymes. In fact, the musical quality of the rhymes will help children refine their auditory discrimination, a skill which is of utmost importance for future reading success.

Children of this age level also have continued need for many read-aloud experiences. Fanciful stories which have generous touches of humor and slighter touches of "ghosts" and other "wild things" are most appealing to this age group. Ample time should also be set aside for verbal interaction so that children may exercise their rapidly developing language abilities.

During the impressionable years children also need to be surrounded with toys that develop their intellectual capacities as well as their manipulative skills. Toys that do everything for the child should be avoided, while toys which require that the child assemble, coordinate, or build the toy into objects or structures should be encouraged. The level of difficulty of such toys should be carefully watched so that children will be challenged but not overly frustrated by the demands of such manipulation and assembly.

Games are important for three- to five-year-olds in two ways: (1) they require group participation and (2) they require the ability to follow simple routines. Children at this age level also need to be introduced to and provided with many art and musical activities to nurture their creative instincts.

In summary, young children need an environment in which reading readiness activities are as varied as the children's curiosity levels. Books and other activities should complement each other during these crucial readiness years.

Reading to Young Children

Young children should be read to daily. This is true for all ages, although the manner and content of the reading change as children approach school age. Children younger than eight months will find the singing of lullabies and nursery rhymes most satisfying. Keep in mind that very young children, from about the age of eight months, thrive on regular schedules and that it is a good practice to set aside a specific time during the day when children are read to. The routine might even include a special place in the home or child care center where the sharing of "words" and books takes place.

The reader should comfortably settle the child on his or her lap before beginning. For children at this age level, singing, reciting, or reading nursery rhymes and engaging in simple fingerplays that make use of the touching of fingers, toes, and noses are the most appropriate activities. Although children from eight to eighteen months still need to hear nursery rhymes and become more involved in fingerplay activities, they are also beginning to show an interest in sharing books. Cloth books or board books that contain illustrations of animals, toys, and food items are most appealing to these children. Children eighteen months and older should be encouraged to help recite familiar nursery rhymes; they should also become more skillful in carrying out familiar fingerplay routines. For children at this age the reader may also start the read-aloud sessions with some brief remarks about the content of the book.

Two-year-olds who are beginning to speak might be encouraged to repeat statements about the book such as, "this is a horse," "the cover is brown." A note of caution: do not substitute or change difficult and unusual words to simpler words. Children thrive on these special words and enjoy letting them roll off their little tongues with great expertise.

When children near the ages of three to five they are ready for daily read-aloud sessions in which the books contain both fanciful and informational stories. The length of the read-aloud sessions may vary, but in any case children should have ample time to talk about the stories as well as make their first attempts at reading them. Any time during the day is suitable for read-aloud and book sharing sessions; however, stories which are shared just before bedtime should probably be more carefully selected so that children will not be frightened or overstimulated. Three- to five-year-olds should also be introduced to family read-aloud sessions so that they will learn to accept group behavior.

Most young children enjoy hearing and looking at the same book over and over again. This habit is part of their great need for established routines. Parents should tolerate this habit and should only gradually entice children to accept many different stories. Keeping this in mind, the reader must, therefore, be patient. The reader can change what might easily become a very monotonous routine into a pleasant one through change of voice and different rates of reading speed. The human voice is a marvelous instrument which can be tuned in many different ways, each of which will enhance and change a story regardless of how many times it has been read. The reader should also never overlook the importance of correct pronunciation, since children will use the reader as the model to be emulated in their own speech development.

Young children also have short attention spans and a reader should not be discouraged if the read-aloud session does not last longer than a few minutes for the very young child. As children grow, so will their attention span, and read-aloud sessions might increase from a few minutes to ten or twenty minutes per day.

The routine of reading aloud might even be changed and enriched through some simple storytelling, without books, of old familiar tales. Storytelling has the special advantage of bringing listener and teller more closely together through constant eye contact and mutual awareness of facial expressions that might otherwise not be possible when the reader has to hold a book.

Even though it was suggested that there are certain advantages to having a set daily routine for reading to children, this does not mean that routines cannot be changed and other places and times be used to read aloud to children. Read-aloud sessions, for instance, may also take place when taking longer trips in the car, when waiting in an office, when going to a picnic, or when going to a park.

Books for special situations. Some children may be helped towards a better understanding of their emotional conflicts after they have had the opportunity to listen to and discuss books that deal with special situations. Books that positively discuss one-parent families, the arrival of a new baby, adopting a new baby, living with a grandparent, the event of death in the family, etc., may help heal or at least soothe some of the conflicts children experience. Books about moving to a new house or going into the hospital could be made available, too.

The best suggestion to give anyone wishing information on time and place to read aloud might be, "Don't let a spare moment pass without catching the opportunity to read to children." That means, of course, "Be prepared!" "Always carry a story in your mind, a book in your pocket." "Use every moment to help your child become a better reader through the best reading readiness program you can provide."

Reading Readiness and the "Special Child"

"Special children" or "exceptional children" are children who might be physically handicapped, emotionally handicapped, or mentally handicapped.

Hearing impaired and deaf children. Contrary to popular belief, hearing impaired children still need to develop some form of auditory discrimination. One way to accomplish this is through much verbal interaction between parent and child. Another method is to expose the hearing impaired and even deaf to many read-aloud experiences. However, the hearing impaired need to be read to by adults whose reading position is at eye level with the listener and in adequate light so the listener can watch the lips of the reader. The reader must also pay considerable attention to facial expression and lip movements because hearing impaired children use both touch and keen observation of face and lips in order to assimilate the verbal material which is being shared with them. The books used with these children must be selected with an awareness that the children need to look at distinct and precise pictures which are representative of objects and scenes that the listener may not be able to discern from the spoken word alone.

Although all reading readiness programs need to include many sensory activities, hearing impaired children need to be involved in even greater numbers of sensory experiences, so that they may develop and strengthen their perceptual skills to compensate for skills in which they are handicapped. An article by Judy Schwartz, showing how to teach reading readiness to hearing impaired children, includes fine examples of how to read, teach fingerplays, and teach unusual words to the hearing impaired. Schwartz also explains how to go about teaching rhythmic activities as well as tactile activities to special children.[12]

Visually impaired children. On the other hand, visually impaired children need to be exposed to an abundance of read-aloud experiences which will help them understand the world they cannot see. The books selected for these children must, therefore, be carefully chosen so that the word pictures are clear and precise and are in keeping with the child's experiential level. Books that deal with abstract ideas should be avoided.

Emotionally disabled children. Children who suffer from emotional problems may also be called "special." At the readiness level these children, frequently referred to as emotionally immature, manifest some of the following behaviors: they cannot get along with their peers; they are subject to frequent temper tantrums; they cry easily when introduced to unfamiliar surroundings; they withdraw from group activities; they show signs of extreme shyness. These behaviors are not always, however, an outgrowth of emotional immaturity. Some children may suffer from emotional problems because they are neglected and abused or live in home environments which do not provide a feeling of being loved and nurtured.

Emotionally immature children who cannot get along with their peers may gain immensely from listening to special books that deal with friendship and how to overcome loneliness. Discussions that grow out of sharing these books should be carefully guided so that children will grow through self-discovery. Children who suffer from extreme shyness may be drawn out of their own shells when they are introduced to read-aloud activities which use books and songs that require both group and individual responses. The use of special music and creative movement may also help these children to overcome their shyness. Children who are in need of love and a feeling of security may enjoy readiness activities which make use of puppets and toys that can be touched and handled. A special measure of security and love can also be created when children are allowed to sit in a magic circle and hold hands with their peers.

Mentally handicapped children. These children may also gain much if they are exposed to a reading readiness program which caters to their more specialized needs. In considering materials and activities for these children it must always be remembered that these children especially need those learning materials and opportunities that deal with concrete experiences. Learning experiences should be relatively brief and also limited in topic content. However, because mentally handicapped children still have interests similar to those of their peers, many can participate in regular group activities.

Minority Children

Some children are also designated "special" because they come from minority backgrounds, from homes in which English is not spoken, or from environments which may be termed disadvantaged because they do not offer children the rearing and nurturing practices which include basic reading readiness skills. Although these children may be categorized as "special" children, they need to develop the very same reading readiness skills that all children should have. In that sense these children are only special because of the manner and degree in which the reading readiness skills should be introduced to them. For example, reading readiness programs which are planned for children as well as parents of non-English speaking homes need first of all to take into consideration the customs of each particular culture. It should be remembered that traditions and cultural barriers might not necessarily allow for eager participation in a program which could seem quite foreign to non-English speaking parents. The language barrier itself could also immediately limit the perimeters of the programs planned for these parents and their children. It should, therefore, become quite obvious that school library media specialists and public librarians may have to work through other agencies which already are very much involved with these children in order to establish contact as well as mutual trust between the homes of minority children and the services that school or public librarians wish to offer.

Readiness Tests

Whether children entering school are ready to learn to read and have achieved the maturity to accomplish the desired skills is usually not checked until children are enrolled in kindergarten classes. At that time a standardized Reading Readiness Test, a relatively informal Readiness Checklist, or both may be used to evaluate the readiness abilities of each child. The tests are usually administered in the Spring so that the test scores will be available for first grade teachers when children enter first grade in the Fall.

Some school districts also offer prekindergarten early childhood programs for children between the ages of three to five who are physically handicapped and/or who experience hearing or vision problems. Children who exhibit signs of poor gross and fine motor skills and who may lack in speech and language development may also qualify for such special programs. Screening for such programs is usually announced by the school districts in the local news media.

Pros and Cons of Reading Readiness Tests

The assessment of reading readiness was begun in the late 1920s with the development of standardized tests. The usefulness and validity of the readiness tests, however, have come under considerable attack in recent years when adverse publicity relating to testing in general appeared in the national media. Because of the lack of confidence in testing by the community at large, school districts are now using standardized tests more guardedly. Tests which were formerly used to predict success or failure are now used as diagnostic tools to assess the areas of strength and weakness.

Some of the better known standardized readiness tests currently used are:

> *Clymer Barrett Prereading Battery.* Princeton, N.J.: Personnel Press.

Test evaluates the child's ability to name letters, match words, discriminate between beginning and ending sounds, ability to match words.

Gates-MacGinitie Reading Tests: Readiness Skills. New York: Teachers College Pr., Columbia Univ.

Test evaluates the child's ability in auditory discrimination, visual discrimination, listening comprehension, and the ability to follow directions.

Houghton-Stroud Reading Readiness Profiles. Boston: Houghton Mifflin.

Test evaluates child's ability in visual discrimination, auditory discrimination, letter naming, using context and auditory clues, identification of the letters of the alphabet.

Metropolitan Readiness Tests. New York: Harcourt Brace Jovanovich.

This test evaluates the child's ability to give word meaning, understanding sentences, matching letters and forms, knowledge of the alphabet. This test also includes the "draw-a-man test."

Murphy-Durrell Diagnostic Reading Readiness Test. New York: Harcourt Brace Jovanovich.

Test evaluates the child's ability in: auditory and visual discrimination, letter name knowledge and learning rate.

A quick overview of the tests indicates that there is some variation of content among them. The variations are even more pronounced in the content and number of subtests that constitute the larger tests and rest ultimately on the inability of test authors to agree about what skills are necessary to learn to read. This means that in every test, some skills are tested and others are not. Some sources have begun to question especially the reliability of the shorter tests.

More and more current research on reading readiness seems to question whether reading readiness test scores can be accepted as predictors of reading success and, in general, to answer negatively. This negative attitude is based on several factors, the one most often cited being the problem exposed by the great variation among the subtests. In constructing subtests authors in too many instances either include or exclude items which might influence the accurate prediction of reading readiness. Another factor is based on recognition that in many instances test authors have assumed that children's readiness experiences are similar and should enable children with similar aptitudes to complete the test with relatively uniform success. This is not always the case. Even if children have had the readiness skills asked for on the test, they may not be able to apply them to the test because of unfamiliarity with the test's terminology or procedures.

The interpretation of the test results also has been questioned. In too many cases the test results have been used exclusively to predict whether children are ready or not, when the results should have also been used as a diagnosis of *why* children are not ready.

Informal Readiness Checklists

Because there is some uncertainty as to the validity of standardized reading readiness tests, some schools supplement them with teacher-prepared reading readiness checklists. These reading readiness checklists, also called informal reading readiness checklists, are gaining in popularity because they can be used more effectively to measure individual ability when the need arises. Although teacher-prepared reading checklists are not necessarily above reproach and their validity can certainly be questioned, they nevertheless provide an excellent means of verifying results which may have been questioned or left unanswered on the standardized test. The preparation of the checklists, of course, requires a sound background in reading readiness diagnostic practices. For teachers who wish to compare their own instruments with other teacher-prepared instruments, there are sample checklists, such as the one which follows, readily available in recent elementary-level reading textbooks.

Informal Reading Readiness Checklist

Satisfactory   Unsatisfactory

1. Oral Language
   a) Can repeat a sentence. "The gray and white cat was frisky."
   b) Can complete a sentence. "A green light means go but a red _____ _____ _____."
   c) Can express self spontaneously.

From Richard J. Smith and Dale D. Johnson, *Teaching Children to Read*, 2nd ed., pp. 38–40. © 1980 by Addison-Wesley, Reading, Massachusetts. Reprinted with permission.

Satisfactory   Unsatisfactory

d) Can make up a simple ending for stories.
e) Can accurately use a large
number of words.
f) Can express self effectively.
2. Listening
a) Can follow simple directions.
b) Can recall a simple sequence
of events.
c) Can recall a story heard.
3. Experiential Background
Can answer questions like the
following:
a) When do you eat breakfast?
b) Whom do you go to when
you're sick?
c) What does a dentist do?
d) Which is bigger, a tree or a
flower?
e) Describe a trip you've made,
in town or out of town.
4. Auditory Discrimination
a) Can hear differences in
words. (same-different)
b) Can hear the length of a
word. (Which is shorter, buy
or happiness?)
c) Can repeat pronounced two-
and three-syllable words.
d) Can hear and repeat sounds
at the beginning, in the middle, and at the end of words.
e) Can discern rhyming from
non-rhyming words.
5. Visual Discrimination
a) Can recognize sizes (big, little, tall, short).
b) Can recognize shapes
(square, round, triangle).
c) Can see differences in unlike
letters.
d) Can see differences in unlike
words.
e) Can match identical letters.
f) Can match identical words.

Satisfactory   Unsatisfactory

6. Perceptual-Motor Skills
   a) Can copy a simple figure.

   b) Can identify left from right
       hand.
   c) Can scan a series of pictures
       from left to right.
   d) Can recognize left-to-right
       sequence of words on a
       page.
   e) Can recognize top-to-bottom
       arrangement of words on a
       page.
   f) Can recognize the left-to-
       right sequence of letters
       within words.
7. Interest
   a) Wants to learn to read.
   b) Likes to be read to.
   c) Is interested in picture
       books.
   d) Is curious about symbols and
       letters.
   e) Seeks out books to take
       home.

Research which compares standardized reading readiness tests with teacher-prepared informal reading readiness checklists is still very scarce. Studies have been published which either describe the failures of the standardized tests[13] or suggest alternative methods to standardized testing.[14]

Library Media Specialists and Reading Readiness

Parents are very much concerned with the reading achievements of their children and want to know how reading failures can be prevented. Responding to the need, public librarians have been offering reading readiness programs for many years. Some of their innovative services have been described in such books as *Start Early for an Early Start* and in articles published in various professional journals through the years. In fact, public librarians have sometimes taken their programs directly to early childhood centers, housing developments, parent training centers, and other places where parents gather to learn more about child development.

Public librarians have not always included the local school system in their programming. This area of service probably was left unserved because public librarians felt it might be more appropriate for school library media specialists and parent-teacher groups (Parent-Teacher Associations or Parent-Teacher Organizations [PTA/PTO]) to initiate such programs. Intimate involvement with children and parents along with sure knowledge of what skills are important for the beginning student make it appropriate for school library media specialists and PTA/PTO to join forces and participate in planning local readiness programs and resources, as well as inform parents about them.

All three—public librarians, school library media specialists, and parent-teacher groups—should constitute the larger team. To get the team approach off the ground, library media specialists, public librarians, and PTA/PTO representatives may wish to schedule an organizational meeting to discuss how a "systems approach" may be implemented. The meetings may be initiated either by a school library media center supervisor or by the head of children's services of a public library. In very large cities and large school districts it may be more practical to call area meetings to keep the number of people attending each meeting to a size that can accommodate a close interchange of ideas. Likewise, in very small school districts and very small library systems, personnel other than supervisors may have to start the process of initiating joint ventures to share readiness information with the community at large.

Where to begin. School library media specialists and public librarians may wish to implement the "systems approach" by calling for an organizational meeting either at the public library or the school library media center. During the meeting specific objectives for a cooperative reading readiness program may be spelled out. For instance, school library media specialists and children's librarians from the public library may wish to consider the development and distribution of reading readiness bibliographies as their first team venture. The PTA/PTO organization can be particularly effective as a distributor of bibliographies to homes within the more immediate school community.

Public librarians, school library media specialists, and the PTA/PTO may also consider cooperating in distributing the bibliographies to groups such as parenting groups and prenatal groups, who have a definite need for bibliographies of this kind. As a team the group may even wish to initiate a special community project of distributing the bibliographies to doctors' offices and hospital maternity wards.

Taking on a far more ambitious project, school library media specialists, public librarians, and the PTA/PTO may consider the possibility of planning workshops or programs for parents that would deal with the need to start reading readiness in the home. Cooperative workshops could deal with such pertinent topics as: when and how to read to preschoolers; selecting the right books for preschoolers; how to develop listening skills in preschoolers.

The manner in which public librarians, school library media specialists, and the PTA/PTO cooperate in developing the programs would depend largely on the extent to which other reading readiness information has been made available to them through other programs. If very little information has been shared with parents, basic presentations may have to be offered several times over the course of several months. However, if parents already have been well informed of the rudiments of reading readiness, only an annual refresher presentation may be needed to keep the reading readiness concept very much alive in everyone's mind.

Parents should leave workshops or presentations with practical, immediately applicable information. For example, school library media specialists may wish to discuss and demonstrate how to share books and related activities with very young children. Public librarians, who are partners in the workshop, may complete the workshop by showing parents materials they can secure at the public library to carry out read-aloud sessions at home. Workshops may also be sponsored by the PTA/PTO, in which guests are the major presenters and school library media specialists and children's librarians from the public library function as resource persons to guide participants to additional resources in the community.

Don't forget the bookstore. The mere distribution of bibliographies is insufficient to get the reading readiness program started in the homes. Bibliographies are only catalysts to help initiate reading activities. What is really needed is for parents to have ready access to the real books so that they are able to carry out the reading activities in their homes. Although many books are available in the public library or school library media center, parents must also learn where books may be purchased. This means, of course, that local bookstores are a very essential part of the overall reading readiness campaign. Bookstore owners may be invited to participate in special workshops or other community programs aimed at spreading reading readiness information. Bookstores, therefore, need to be constantly supplied with updated bibliographies and information on reading readiness programs in the community. For all practical reasons bookstores need to have the bibliographies as early as possible so that they may have the books on their shelves when the programs take place.

At the book fair. Book fairs sponsored through the cooperative efforts of school library media specialists and the PTA/PTO, whose aim is to sell books, mainly paperbacks, to children and parents, can also be used effectively to promote the sale of reading readiness materials.

Reading readiness books selected for the fair should be ordered to arrive separately from the other books. In this way, the readiness books may be immediately segregated from the other book fair materials and then displayed separately from the general display in a special corner. The investment of a few additional dollars for special, eye-catching posters and banners may very well draw additional attention to this all-important display.

The reading readiness display should also receive special publicity in the book fair's advertising campaign, which might include a write-up in the local paper or a special spot announcement on the local radio or TV station. A special guest who is knowledgeable about reading readiness might also be invited to be present at the readiness display. Such a guest will provide that special perception of authority as well the touch that means "We really care" to the overall program.

Library media specialists who have not sponsored a book fair may wish to consult the *Elementary School Librarian's Almanac* for the pertinent details which need to be considered, including how to select a book jobber to furnish the books; how to publicize the fair; and how to set up sales routines for the day of the event.

School library media specialists in schools that have not yet established a parent-teacher organization may have to take it upon themselves to approach the school staff and promote the idea of a yearly reading readiness workshop. This is particularly recommended if a school or school district has experienced many reading failures. A sound reading readiness program should be vigorously promoted if the school is looking for solutions on how to prevent future reading failures.

How to Prepare Bibliographies for Parents

The following suggestions can help busy school library media specialists prepare effective reading readiness bibliographies for distribution to parents.

1. Keep the bibliography short. 10 to 15 books will be adequate.
2. Limit the age span of the children for which each bibliography is prepared. Most users prefer something precise.
3. Bibliographies to be distributed to parents and other community agencies should suggest books that are readily available in local bookstores.
4. Select books that are available both in paper and hardcover. Cost is a very important factor for many homes.
5. Annotate books very briefly and precisely. A touch of humor will be appreciated.
6. Take the time and prepare bibliographies which are attractive. Worn out ditto sheets will not do.

Selecting Books for Reading Readiness: Suggestions

Age 0 to 24 months

1. Search for books which are made either of cloth or very substantial paper or cardboard. Cloth books are best for this age level. (A note of caution: at this age level books will frequently be tasted by the reader. Paper and inks should be nonpoisonous.)
2. Size of book should be considered carefully. Small hands should have access to some small books which they can hold and manipulate with ease. Some large-size books should also be included. These books can be shared between parent and child during story hours. Large-size books also present concepts in more recognizable manner.
3. Select books which introduce familiar objects such as pets, toys, objects from the nursery and home.
4. Select books which have large illustrations with distinct outlines. One or two items per page will make it easier for the very young to develop visual perception.
5. Select illustrations with distinct bright colors. The very young will begin to learn to identify basic colors from these illustrations.
6. Select books which have a very simple and very short uncomplicated story line. The main concept should be repeated throughout the story.
7. Select books with large print.

Age 24 to 36 months. Continue to use the suggestions for the preceding age level and add the following considerations:

1. Select picture books which have distinct pictures and narrative of one to two sentences per page. Words of the text should be repetitive so that children may have many opportunities to participate in retelling the story.
2. Search for nursery tale collections that are very simple and very short. Tales dealing with animals and food are most appropriate for this age child.
3. Include alphabet books which show one letter or one word per page and use familiar objects such as toys, animals, clothing. The illustrations which accompany the text should be large and have distinct outlines. Special attention should also be paid to the sound of the letter and the word in which the sound is used. This is particularly true for vowel sounds. The letter "i" should be demonstrated through a word using the sound "i" as in "ice," but NOT the word "insect."

Age 3 to 5 years

1. Search for picture books which feature basic concepts such as colors, shapes, sounds, and laterality through distinct illustrations and a one- or two-sentence text per page.
2. Select picture books which present factual information on nature, animals, seasons, family, growing up, and getting along with others through distinct illustrations and a precise text. Format of book should encourage young children to become involved in the exploration of information and to ask additional questions about the topic.
3. Select alphabet books which include both the letter and whole word in phrases which reiterate the letter several times. The use of alliteration will help children make letter-sound associations. Those that mainly use pictures as clues for the letter are also recommended to help children develop their visual acuity as well as practice their vocabulary knowledge. The alphabet books that show only part of the object on one page and the complete object on the next page, thereby involving children in a guessing game, are excellent to stimulate children's intellectual curiosity. And, alphabet books that use either fine artistic illustrations or black-and-white photographs also are appropriate for this age level.
4. In selecting counting books, look for clear illustrative representation of number groupings. At this age level it is best

to select books which use only one object or concept to demonstrate counting from 1 to 10.

5. Search for "I Can Read" books which tell a story through a one sentence per page format. Illustrations which accompany the text should serve the young reader as picture clues.

6. Select read-aloud picture books which have main characters who experience problems with which young children can identify. Problems such as being too small, being neglected because of younger or older siblings, being afraid, being disobedient, wishing for special animals or toys are topics which appeal to this age group.

7. Search for read-aloud books which are fanciful and have such main characters as "friendly ghosts," animals who pretend they are ferocious but actually are friendly, and toys which overcome difficult situations.

8. Include a few "small" books to be handled by very small hands.

9. Select wordless picture books which inform the child or tell a basic story through precise colorful illustrations. These are excellent books for developing a child's imagination, visual acuity, and language facility.

Books for "Special Children"

In developing bibliographies for "special children" consult with experts in each specific area. Make a listing of the specific needs for these special children. Based on the needs, select books which can meet the special requirements through illustration and text. Special nonprint media may also be selected to help these children achieve their readiness tasks.

Also consult the following sources for help in the selection process:

Baskin, Barbara Holland, and Harris, Karen H., eds. *The Special Child in the Library.* Chicago: American Library Association, 1976. Includes information on how to serve emotionally disturbed and socially maladjusted as well as hearing and visually impaired children.

Butler, Dorothy. *Cushla and Her Books.* Boston: The Horn Book, Inc., 1980.

Dreyer, Sharon Spredeman. *The Bookfinder: A Guide to Children's Literature about the Needs and Problems of Youth Age 2–15.* Circle Pines, Minn.: American Guidance Service, Inc., 1981.

Gillis, Ruth J. *Children's Books for Times of Stress: An Annotated* Bibliography. Bloomington, Ind.: Indiana Univ. Pr., 1978. Includes suggestions for preschoolers.

Thomas, Carol H., and Thomas, James L., eds., *Meeting the Needs of the Handicapped: A Resource for Teachers and Librarians.* Phoenix: Oryx Pr., 1980. Includes excellent descriptions of all types of handicapped children plus descriptions of library-based learning activities.

Wallick, Mollie Marcus, "An Autistic Child and Books," *Top of the News* 37:69–76 (Fall 1980). Includes bibliography of books which were used with autistic child age four years and five months.

Sample Reading Readiness Bibliography to Give to Parents

Age 0 to 24 months

The Animal's Ark; il. by Marlies Merk Najaka. Elsevier/Dutton, 1979. A strong colorful book which will keep your child busy while attending church.

Brown, Marc. *Finger Rhymes.* Dutton, 1980. Simple rhymes accompany the large black-and-white illustrations and small simple inserts which demonstrate how to use fingers to carry out the activities.

Chorao, Kay. *The Baby's Lap Book.* Dutton, 1977. A collection of nursery rhymes especially appropriate for this age group. Black-and-white illustrations on pink and yellow paper lend a traditional touch.

Johnson, John E. *The Me Book.* Random, 1979. A soft, washable, nontoxic book which will help one-year-olds describe themselves.

Pfloog, Jan. *Puppies.* Random, 1979. Puppies eat, play, chase, and even argue in this very solid, hard-to-destroy book for the very young.

Scarry, Richard. *Huckle's Book.* Random, 1979. With the help of the little gold bug Huckles learns to describe all the members of the family. Soft and washable.

Age 24 to 36 months

Carle, Eric. *My Very First Book of Words.* Crowell, 1974. A challenging word book for children who are beginning to recognize a few sight words.

Crews, Donald. *Truck.* Greenwillow, 1980. Bright colors, large illustrations, and large lettering relate information about transportation. A fine book to develop visual perception.

Hutchins, Pat. *Rosie's Walk.* Macmillan, 1968. A very fine read-aloud book where child and reader can interact and help solve the chase between unperturbed hen and fox.

Smollin, Michael. *Learning Colors with Strawberry Shortcake.* Random, 1980. A small book for small hands and bright minds who want to discover all about colors.

Wells, Rosemary. *Max's Ride.* Dial, 1979. A boardbook explaining the concept of location.

Age 3 to 5 years

Barton, Byron. *Building a House.* Greenwillow, 1981. Bright illustrations and one-sentence explanations enlighten the very young on how a house is being constructed.

Chess, Victoria. *Alfred's Alphabet Walk.* Greenwillow, 1979. An alphabet book for children who know their basic letters and look for new challenges.

De Regniers, Beatrice Schenk. *May I Bring a Friend?* il. by Beni Montresor. Atheneum, 1964. A read-aloud book which has enough refrains to encourage children to help tell the story.

Gretz, Susanna. *Teddy Bears 1 to 10.* Follett, 1969. Large numbers and cuddly teddy bears combined with imaginative language make this a most attractive first counting book.

Hoban, Tana. *Is It Red? Is It Yellow? Is It Blue?* Greenwillow, 1978. Wordless picture book which entices children to become aware of colors through the use of objects and places with which children are familiar.

Notes

1. Lloyd O. Ollila, ed., *Handbook for Administrators and Teachers: Reading in the Kindergarten* (Newark, Del.: International Reading Ass., 1980), p. 4.
2. Edward Fry, *Elementary Reading Instruction* (New York: McGraw-Hill, 1977), p. 111.
3. Fry, *Elementary Reading Instruction*, p. 112.
4. Dolores Durkin, *Teaching Young Children to Read*, 3rd ed. (Boston: Allyn and Bacon, 1980), p. 64.
5. Ibid.
6. Ibid.
7. Durkin, *Teaching Young Children*, p. 52.
8. Susanna Pflaum-Connor, *The Development of Language and Reading in Young Children*, 2nd ed. (Columbus, Ohio: Charles E. Merrill, 1978), p. 133.
9. Jerome S. Bruner, *The Process of Education* (New York: Vintage Books, 1960), p. 33.
10. Ferne Johnson, ed., *Start Early for an Early Start* (Chicago: American Library Assn., 1976).
11. Richard J. Smith and Dale D. Johnson, *Teaching Children to Read*, 2nd ed. (Reading, Mass.: Addison-Wesley, 1980), pp. 27–28.
12. Judy I. Schwartz, "Reading Readiness for the Hearing Impaired," *Academic Therapy* 25: 65–75 (Sept. 1979).
13. Smith and Johnson, *Teaching Children to Read*, 2nd ed., pp. 38–40.
14. Vito Perrone, "Alternatives to Standardized Testing," *National Elementary Principal* 54:96–101 (July/Aug. 1975).

2

Reading at the
Kindergarten Level

The reading process takes a giant step forward when children enter kindergarten. Reading readiness skills such as auditory discrimination, visual discrimination, conceptual skills, oral language skills, and eye-hand coordination skills that have been introduced informally at home or in child care centers, or even through such television programs as Sesame Street, will now be reinforced and enhanced in a more structured program.

The program itself is more structured in that kindergarten classes are not only situated within a formal school environment, they are also subject to the educational goals and objectives prescribed by the state board of education and the standards set forth by the local school board. Kindergarten classes usually meet only on a half-day schedule. This means kindergarten teachers are responsible for a morning and an afternoon session. Instructional routines are the same for both. A typical kindergarten day might include the following activities:

> The teacher greets the children and gathers them to discuss the name of the day, the name of the month, and the weather conditions of the day. Special events, holidays, and birthdays may also be celebrated during this period.
>
> Children disperse to special interest centers such as the housekeeping center, art center, language center, math–science center, library center, music center, manipulative center, and toy center.
>
> Group meeting for special indoor or outdoor playtime, nap, and milk break.
>
> Group meeting for storytime and music time, and/or rhythmic activities. Storytimes may occur twice during each kindergarten period.
>
> Getting ready to go home.

Although daily routines remain essentially the same through-out the entire school year, the learning activities usually increase in difficulty as the year progresses. For instance, oral language de-velopment and conceptual skills may be encouraged and practiced during conversation time as well as storytime. Auditory discrimi-nation may be especially emphasized during music and song time as well as storytime. The auditory skills may, furthermore, be encouraged through listening to tapes and records which may have been placed either in the language center or school library media center. Visual discrimination may be practiced in the lan-guage center through activities that require children to match shapes or letters. They may also be asked to match pictures and words.

During the latter part of the year children may actually be asked to complete some simple worksheets. Eye-hand coordina-tion and gross and fine motor skills are usually reinforced and developed through activities planned for the kindergarten chil-dren in the manipulative center. These skills may also be practiced by playing special games which involve handling, catching, and throwing various sized balls. Gross and fine motor skills may also be enhanced through dance and other rhythmic activities. It is in the school library media center where all the acquired reading readi-ness skills are put to work and where children are encouraged to take that enormously big step and begin to read the books which have been carefully and lovingly selected for their first reading encounters.

Materials and Methods

Materials and methods used to introduce reading readiness in the kindergarten classroom vary greatly from district to district. Many schools use reading readiness materials that are provided as part of the same basal reader package as will be used through the primary years. This approach has several distinct advantages. One is that it provides for continuity in the reading program from kindergarten through grade six or eight. Another advantage is that it keeps teachers well informed of the sequence of skills development from grade level to grade level. In addition, commercially prepared texts generally require the teacher to spend less time preparing for class. Many basal programs include enrichment materials such as story boards, story boxes, books, filmstrips, and audio cassettes. These materials are especially welcomed by teachers who have limited access to other enrichment materials within their schools.

Some schools supplement their basal program kindergarten materials with other commercially prepared reading readiness materials in order to meet the special reading readiness needs of their students. School districts that have many entering children with very limited oral language development often use supplementary materials, such as the Peabody Language Development Kits. School districts that must provide for kindergarten children with extremely wide ranges of readiness abilities may supplement their regular readiness program with the SRA Reading Program, which provides for both children who excel and children who fall short in their readiness abilities.

Although there are many advantages to commercially prepared programs, there are also certain pronounced disadvantages. Programs that are too structured can easily become inflexible and prevent teacher and children from spontaneously taking advantage of learning opportunities. Commercially prepared programs also may prevent teachers from using their own creativity in reaching children of various learning needs and abilities. These programs frequently neglect to promote the school library media center as the place where the "real" reading materials can be found to support and enrich the readiness program.

Recognizing some of the shortcomings of the commercially prepared readiness programs, many school districts across the nation are developing their own readiness programs and materials, based on their own community's needs. This approach has certain advantages since it enables teachers to select instructional methods and materials more suitable to meet the learning needs of their children.

For instance, in cases where children lack visual discrimination skills, the teacher may bring in everyday objects to help children become more visually perceptive of the world around them. Likewise, when children need to develop their auditory skills, the teacher may use examples of sounds from the world in which they live. Teacher-prepared materials are also more effective since they generally stress concrete rather than abstract objects. Concreteness is important because a great deal of learning at this stage of development still needs to take place through sensory experiences of concrete objects. Commercially prepared materials are necessarily limited to more abstract paper and pencil learning/teaching methods, which children at this stage of development find more difficult to comprehend.

Although teacher-prepared programs are only as good as teachers are willing and able to make them, they usually are more personal and flexible in meeting the needs of children with various abilities and cultural backgrounds. Teacher-prepared programs also take greater advantage of the services and materials available to them in their own school library media centers. In this way, children are immediately introduced to materials that suit their particular needs, rather than the needs of a majority.

How Structured Should a Kindergarten Program Be?

How formal and how structured reading readiness programs should be have been subjects of controversy. The lack of guidelines has brought about some tension not only within the educational community, but also between the educational community and the parent community.

In order to circumvent further serious misunderstanding, a committee was formed by the American Association of Elementary/Kindergarten/Nursery Educators, the Association for Childhood Education International, the Association for Supervision and Curriculum Development, the International Reading Association, the National Association for the Education of Young Children, the National Association of Elementary School Principals, and the National Council of Teachers of English. This committee issued a joint statement, "Reading and Pre-First Grade," which follows in its entirety. The recommendations it makes are of vital importance to school library media specialists who need to formulate objectives in developing cooperative reading readiness programs for their communities.

Reading and Pre-First Grade

A Perspective on Pre-First Graders and the Teaching of Reading

Pre-first graders need opportunities to express orally, graphically, and dramatically their feelings and responses to experiences, opportunities to interpret the language of others whether it is written, spoken, or non-verbal.

Teachers of pre-first graders need preparation which emphasizes developmentally appropriate language experiences for all pre-first graders, including those ready to read or already reading, the combined efforts of professional organizations, colleges, and universities to help them successfully meet the concerns outlined in this document.

Concerns

1. A growing number of children are enrolled in pre-kindergarten and kindergarten classes in which highly structured pre-reading and reading programs are being used.
2. Decisions related to schooling, including the teaching of reading, are increasingly being made on economic and political bases instead of on our knowledge of young children and of how they best learn.
3. In a time of diminishing financial resources, schools often try to make "a good showing" on measures of achievement that may or may not be appropriate for the children involved. Such measures all too often dictate the content and goals of the programs.
4. In attempting to respond to pressures for high scores on widely-used measures of achievement, teachers of young children sometimes feel compelled to use materials, methods, and activities designed for older children. In so doing, they may impede the development of intellectual functions such as curiosity, critical thinking, and creative expression, and, at the same time, promote negative attitudes toward reading.
5. A need exists to provide alternative ways to teach and evaluate progress in pre-reading and reading skills.
6. Teachers of pre-first graders who are carrying out highly individualized programs without depending upon commercial readers and workbooks need help in articulating for themselves and the public what they are doing and why.

Recommendations

1. Provide reading experiences as an integrated part of the broader communication process that includes listening, speaking, and writing. A language experience approach is an example of such integration.
2. Provide for a broad range of activities both in scope and in content. Include direct experiences that offer opportunities to communicate in different settings with different persons.
3. Foster children's affective and cognitive development by providing materials, experiences, and opportunities to communicate what they know and how they feel.
4. Continually appraise how various aspects of each child's total development affects his/her reading development.
5. Use evaluative procedures that are developmentally appropriate for the children being assessed and that reflect the goals and objectives of the instructional program.
6. Insure feelings of success for all children in order to help them see themselves as persons who can enjoy exploring language and learning to read.

7. Plan flexibly in order to accommodate a variety of learning styles and ways of thinking.
8. Respect the language the child brings to school, and use it as a base for language activities.
9. Plan activities that will cause children to become active participants in the learning process rather than passive recipients of knowledge.
10. Provide opportunities for children to experiment with language and simply to have fun with it.
11. Require that pre-service and in-service teachers of young children be prepared in the teaching of reading in a way that emphasizes reading as an integral part of the language arts as well as the total curriculum.
12. Encourage developmentally appropriate language learning opportunities in the home.

The School Library Media Specialist in the Kindergarten Readiness Program

The role of school library media specialists in the kindergarten reading readiness program is to assist teachers, children, parents, and the community at large by promoting reading readiness. When helping teachers, school library media specialists function as "team teachers." When helping children, they function in what might best be referred to at this level as "enchanters" of reading. When helping parents and the community at large, school library media specialists function also as resource and public relations specialists.

The School Library Media Specialist as Team Teacher

School library media specialists become team teachers when they share with kindergarten teachers teaching ideas and methods that make use of books and other materials available through the library media center. The team teaching program can best be initiated through conferences in which teachers and library media specialists address questions of mutual concern. The concerns may be resolved through the suggestion of special teaching ideas, examples of which follow.

IDEA: How to use picture books to help reluctant participants. Library media specialists asked by kindergarten teachers for help in stimulating children who are reluctant participants in reading readiness activities may suggest the use of some participation books. Mirra Ginsburg's *Good Morning, Chick* is a fine starter book for participatory activities. It is packed with phrases and ideas upon which valuable teaching ideas can be based and with which to entice even the most reluctant child to become more involved in group activities. To begin with, the simple refrain, "like this," which is repeated throughout the entire book, can be repeated both by the entire class at once and by individual children who need to be called on so that they become more attentive and involved in their group's activities.

The next step is to alert children to seek out more difficult refrains scattered throughout the book. At first, the teacher might help in the search and ask students to repeat them as a group. In later readings individal children might be called upon to respond with the appropriate refrain.

Even though the book may seem amazingly simple at first glance, it is packed with things and events of great interest to kindergarten children. The hatching of a chick, the caring for the chick by a speckled mother hen, and the chick's learning how to survive in a barnyard filled with intimidating black cats and puddles too deep for tiny chicks can lead to many other reading and talking experiences which might appeal to students who have so far only been reluctant participants. The inclusion of words such as "speckled," "coddled," and "hissed" helps to develop a sense of language in the listeners. Even the large, bright illustrations include a few specific references to color concepts that can be used for teaching/learning purposes.

Another book that is excellent for stimulating children's participatory spirits and their listening habits is *May I Bring a Friend?* by Beatrice Schenk De Regniers. Its rhymes and intricate refrains make it necessary for children to listen diligently so that they will be able to call out the various days of the week, the names of the animal guests, and the menu items. The imaginative theme of the book also provides many more teaching opportunities. A unit could be developed on zoo animals. Another unit on "real kings and queens" could even be initiated. As a grand finale the teacher might bring along several boxes of animal crackers and invite the children to a real classroom party wearing their special handmade crowns. Such a party could even be held in the library media center.

Another book particularly suitable for helping children become active participants, which is also useful in developing their listening and visual skills, is entitled *I Know Something You Don't Know*. Maria Enrica Agostinelli is its author. The fun of guessing what the objects—which appear incomplete on one page and completed on the next—might be will make even the most inattentive child listen and look carefully.

Other books that challenge the listening and visual skills of students are Roger Bester's *Guess What?* and Janina Domanska's *What Do You See?* Bester uses black-and-white photographs to entice viewers to find the answer to the repeated question, "What has . . . ?" in the animal world. To answer the question, participants have to use their visual as well as auditory skills to come up with the correct answer. Domanska shows the young audience that the world can be seen from many different perspectives and that what one animal finds useful might be quite useless to another. Books like these, which deal with important information in a most enticing manner, can also be used as cornerstones for units that delve into such topics as animal classification, animals and their habitats, and animal behavior. What started out as a simple participatory exercise may, with proper planning, turn into a learning exercise that will attract not only the affective but also the cognitive involvement of the participants.

When selecting books to encourage active participation, do not overlook Marjorie Flack's *Ask Mr. Bear*, John Langstaff's *Over in the Meadow*, Wanda Gág's *Millions of Cats*, Françoise's *Jeanne-Marie Counts Her Sheep*, and Paul Galdone's *The Three Billy Goats Gruff* and *The Three Bears*. The musical refrains in each of these books will soon take hold of even the most reluctant participants, and it won't be long before they, too, will want to chime in and repeat such wonderful words as, "trip, trap, trip, trap," or "millions, billions, and trillions." Even the children who are already familiar with some of these books through prior storytime experiences may appreciate that touch of familiarity which can encourage them to take the big step and become active participants.

IDEA: How to use books and AV materials to develop listening skills. Individual conferences with kindergarten teachers may be used to tell them about other resources, such as tapes and records, which can be used to improve listening skills. Songs, music, and rhythmic activities are very important components of any reading readiness program. By listening to a tape or record featuring action songs, such as *Be-a-Train*, children are encouraged to listen, follow directions, and respond with creative movements. Records of popular and classical music may also be suggested, to help children in kindergarten develop abilities to listen critically and creatively. Listening skills must be enhanced constantly in order to help kindergarten children develop auditory acuity, so that they may be well prepared to distinguish among the various sound patterns found in the English language.

School library media specialists may also wish to acquaint kindergarten teachers with the various song books that may be checked out through the library. Picture books based on songs, such as the Emberleys' delightful presentation of *Simon's Song*, Aliki's tenderly illustrated folk lullaby, *Hush Little Baby*, or Robert Quackenbush's so humorously illustrated *Go Tell Aunt Rhody*, should be mentioned too. Books like these make for very rewarding singing and listening experiences.

IDEA: How to use wordless picture books to develop visual acuity. Since the development of visual acuity is so very important for reading success, library media specialists definitely want to suggest to their teachers the use of picture books that, being wordless, tell a story through pictures alone or of picture books with only a limited text. Books such as Pat Hutchins's *Rosie's Walk*, Tana Hoban's *Is It Red? Is It Yellow? Is It Blue?* and *Look Again!*, Brinton Turkle's *Deep in the Forest*, and Raymond Briggs's *The Snowman* are only a few examples that can be used most effectively—books that teach children both to look for details when looking at pictures and to use the details to interpret the story line.

Once kindergarten children have begun to make progress in developing visual acuity, they are ready for books in whose pictures are objects hidden within other objects. Among books that fall into this more advanced category are *Changes, Changes* by Pat Hutchins, *Snail, Where Are You?* and *One, Two, Where's My Shoe?* by Tomi Ungerer, *Apples* by Nonny Hogrogian, *Each Peach Pear Plum* by Janet and Allan Ahlberg, and *But Where Is the Green Parrot?* by Wanda Zacharias. These and the previously discussed less complicated books are all highly recommended, for not only do they develop visual acuity, but each develops additional reading readiness skills through its pictures and story line.

For instance, in Pat Hutchins's *Rosie's Walk*, Rosie is used to introduce such difficult concepts as "over," "around," "across," and "past" in order to get the hen safely through the barnyard. Tana Hoban's book, *Look Again!* shows children that colors are all around them through striking color photographs. Similar lessons can be taught with the Zacharias book, *But Where Is The Green Parrot?* which uses the parrot to identify familiar objects in unfamiliar settings. A similar lesson is taught by the Ahlbergs in their book, *Each Peach Pear Plum*, which makes use of familiar nursery tales and rhymes to help children discover the hiding places of the main characters. All of these books urge children to become imaginative as well as careful observers.

IDEA: Using the opaque projector with books in the classroom. It is of great importance that all children have an equal opportunity to participate in the critical visual skill development lessons that are offered with books. School library media specialists might suggest that teachers use the opaque projector to introduce some of these books to their classes. By means of this audiovisual aid, the teacher is able to provide every member of the class better visual access to the illustrations of the book.

IDEA: How to keep early readers happy. Many children enter their kindergarten classrooms with a basic sight vocabulary acquired during their preschool years. This important basic sight vocabulary should by no means be neglected; it should be encouraged and built on in any way possible with books that will challenge the budding zest for reading.

Books such as Dennis Panek's *Detective Whoo*, which has only one word per page, or Robert Kalan's *Rain*, which progresses from one word to a sentence of five words, are examples of fine starter books which will satisfy a kindergartner's most urgent desire to be able to read a book all by himself or herself.

Children with more extensive word backgrounds will be ready for such books as Betsy Maestro's *Harriet Reads Signs and More Signs*, Shigeo Watanabe's *Get Set Go!* and *What a Good Lunch*, Cindy Wheeler's *A Good Day, A Good Night*, Ann Rockwell's *Honk Honk!* Judi Barrett's *Animals Should Definitely Not Act like People*, John Stadler's *Cat at Bat*, Vicky Shiefman's *M Is for Move*, Richard Scarry's *Lowly Worm Word Book*, and Dr. Seuss's *I Can Read with My Eyes Shut!* Rosemary Wells's sturdy "Very First Book" series featuring Ruby and Max and their first word adventures in *Max's First Word*, *Max's New Suit*, and *Max's Ride* can also be highly recommended for children with some word knowledge.

A note of caution is called for at this point since it must be stressed that only children who express a desire or readiness for reading should be introduced to books that they can read on their own. Reading at this level should be an enjoyable experience and completely voluntary, never mandatory. This is a crucial moment at which children can become either eager readers or reluctant ones because we either have inundated them with the right materials or hampered them with readiness activities which they had already outgrown before entering the classroom.

IDEA: How to be ready with materials for teachers. Make up a card for each book that you find particularly suitable for special teaching/learning ideas. This card can be duplicated and laminated and kept in a resource file to be used over and over again for many years. Ordering duplicate copies of books for which file cards have been developed is a good idea. These books can be placed on special shelves, readily available to the teacher when need arises.

Format of card:

```
PARTICIPATION BOOKS/Kindergarten level

Ginsburg, Mirra.        Good Morning, Chick.
                        Illustrated by Byron Barton.
                        Greenwillow, 1980

Teaching ideas:        Use refrains
                       Use rhyming words

Concepts:              Hatching of chick
                       Survival of young chick
                       Introduction of colors

Language:              speckled, fluffy, coddled
```

Workshops for Teachers

The presentation of workshops has certain advantages because a large number of people can be introduced at one time to the services and materials available in the school library media center. Workshops can be scheduled at any time during the year. Since time is precious to both teachers and library media specialists, it is suggested that a workshop last no longer than 40 to 60 minutes. Workshops for kindergarten teachers may be on topics such as "Using wordless picture books to stimulate oral language activities," "Learning number concepts through picture books," "How to use the overhead projector to learn the ABCs," and "How to keep the early reader reading." The ultimate success of any workshop will depend on how carefully the objectives have been set and how precisely they are followed during the actual presentation. How to prepare a workshop and how to select other pertinent topics will be discussed in chapter 9.

The School Library Media Specialist as Enchanter of Reading

"To enchant" means to sing and chant and that is exactly what library media specialists must do. They must sing and chant to kindergarten children. What is more, they must sing and chant about the joys of reading at every opportunity. They must sing and chant old nursery rhymes and folktales. They must sing and chant the more modern tales of humor and adventure, and they must sing and chant about the books that contain information to satisfy the curiosity of the young listener. Of all the tasks that school library media specialists have to accomplish, the task of "enchanter of reading" must certainly be the most rewarding because it affords every library media specialist the opportunity to put in the foundation upon which kindergarten children can build a successful reading career.

Putting in a foundation is a most demanding job. The school library media specialist should, therefore, be meticulous in selecting materials to share with kindergarten children. Only the very best is good enough for children who are still in their most impressionable years. Read-aloud books should be selected not because they are "cute," but rather because they contain words to stir listeners' minds into action and illustrations to appeal to children's creative instincts and stimulate more perceptive and imaginative thinking.

In story hours, children experience not only the joys of listening to books but also the immeasurable opportunities which can come through the ability to read books. Although story hours should never take on the appearance or structure of formal classroom instruction, they can nevertheless promote and reinforce the reading readiness skills introduced in the classroom.

In planning story hours school library media specialists should consider opening and closing each session with special activities to enhance certain basic reading readiness skills. Story hours might be opened and closed with simple fingerplays, nursery rhymes, alphabet books, number books, or concept books to promote and reinforce certain skills.

Fingerplays are most effective in helping young children to develop gross and fine motor skills. Moreover, they help children to learn to listen and to follow directions. This is a readiness skill which every child must master in order to become a skillful reader. Nursery rhymes are still the best means to help children develop their auditory acuity, a sense of language, and a sense for rhyme. The development of all these skills will prepare them for phonic instruction. The value of alphabet books on all topics and in all shapes and formats can never be stressed enough when it comes to reading readiness. Kindergarten children, in particular, must constantly be made aware that the letters of the alphabet, which are introduced in the classroom rather abstractly as singular letters on the chalkboard or ditto sheet, can actually turn into words on a page in a book.

Read-aloud experiences can also enrich the vocabulary of kindergarten children. Kindergarten children who possess only limited speaking and listening vocabularies are usually very handicapped when they begin their formal reading program. School library media specialists aware of classrooms with many children with limited speaking abilities should select books that encourage participation for the story hours of those classrooms. This gives children the experience of acquiring new words and language fluency so that they will begin to speak with greater self-confidence.

In planning library visits by kindergarten children librarians may wish to limit the visit to thirty minutes. Of that time fifteen minutes may be used to read one longer story or two shorter stories. A few minutes also need to be set aside to settle children in for the read-aloud experience as well as ready them for an orderly return to their classrooms. Approximately five to six weeks into the semester, when children have learned to print their own names, they may begin to check out one or two books. For this practice library media specialists need to set aside at least ten to fifteen minutes so that children have time to browse and select books as well as check them out.

Although most children are eager and want to learn to read, there are some children who need the extra touch of enchantment to become interested in undertaking this rather demanding yet rewarding learning effort. Some of these reluctant readers may come from homes where parents pay little attention to the educational needs of their children. Occasionally children will also be reluctant readers because they simply have not reached the level of intellectual maturity that would allow them to concentrate on abstract learning activities for relatively long periods of time. Some children may also be reluctant readers because their read-aloud experience is so limited that they are unable to follow the stories shared with them. They are the children who will need a special touch of enchantment to keep them from becoming early reading failures. The main message for these children must ultimately be that success in reading is worth all the painful effort they have to put forth. In cases where special programming is called for, school library media specialists can search for additional enchanters to provide these in-depth services; for example, a grandparent enchanter program might be suggested.

A few tips on how to enchant. The success of the read-aloud sessions will depend largely on how enchanters sing and chant their songs. At the kindergarten level it is very important that the stories be read slowly enough that young listeners can absorb their content. The enunciation and pronunciation of the words should receive careful attention. The pitch and tone of voice should be kept at a moderate level, not too high or too low. Careful timing of reading speed will enable the reader to induce elements of mystery and suspense. If the enchanter ends each reading with a carefully prepared ending—but *never* asks, "How did you like the story?"— the final audience response will be greater. It is good to pause for a minute and let the children dream and think about the material just presented, then to allow a period of discussion, if the children are ready for it.

Where picture books have very small illustrations but a strong story line, it is best for the illustrations not to be shared until the story has been completed. The enchanter might even tell the audience that the illustrations will not be shown until the end to prevent undue commotion and questioning by the children. By following these tips, school library media specialists will become the very best enchanters of reading and thereby help children accept reading as a most exciting and rewarding task, one they will want to accomplish.

The Library Media Specialist as Resource and Public Relations Person for Parents

School library media specialists are resource persons for parents. In this role, they can inform and guide parents on helping children to become successful readers through a read-aloud program at home. A carefully planned presentation sponsored through the school PTA/PTO organization will probably reach the greatest number of parents. The presentation itself does not need to be long but it should be succinct. The following points may be considered for a program: how to select the right books, the advantages of borrowing books from public libraries, how and when to read to children, and where to read to children. The distribution of a bibliography to help parents make their first book choices and get them off to a successful reading start can conclude the presentation. A short bibliography attractively prepared with annotations that beckon the reader to reach for the books will have far greater appeal than a long bibliography printed from old, worn-out ditto sheets. A sample bibliography appears at the end of this chapter.

Keeping a community resource file for parents who need to know where to get help for special problems that children might encounter during their readiness program is another service of the school library media specialist as resource person. The establishment and upkeep of the community resource file can be carried out cooperatively among the school library media center, the public library, and other participating community agencies.

Sample Reading Readiness Bibliography
to be Handed Out to Parents

Asbjornsen, P. C., and J. E. Moe. *The Three Billy Goats Gruff*; il. by Marcia Brown. Harcourt, 1957. The story of an ugly troll and some very smart goats. The whole family can participate in telling this story.

Burningham, John. *Mr. Gumpy's Outing*. Holt, 1970. Children can help tell this story of Mr. Gumpy and his boating trip with a menagerie of cantankerous animals.

Burton, Virginia Lee. *The Little House*. Houghton, 1942. A quiet story of a little house that was nearly lost in the big city.

Carrick, Carol. *The Foundling*; il. by Donald Carrick. Seabury, 1977. The heart-warming story of a little boy who has a hard time selecting a new dog after his old friend was killed.

DePaola, Tomie. *Nana Upstairs Nana Downstairs*; il. by the author. Putnam, 1973. A tender story of a little boy's great love for a great-grandmother and grandmother.

Freeman, Don. *Corduroy*. Viking, 1968. An adventure story of a bear, a missing button, a department store, and a little girl who needed a friend, even though he was not quite perfect.

Gág, Wanda. *Millions of Cats*. Coward, 1928. A perfect story for children who want to adopt every stray that comes their way.

Hoban, Russell. *Bedtime for Frances*; il. by Garth Williams. Harper, 1960. A delightful story for all children who like to delay going to bed.

Krasilovsky, Phyllis. *The Man Who Didn't Wash His Dishes*; il. by Barbara Cooney. Doubleday, 1950. A humorous tale of a man who found a new way to finally wash all of his dishes.

Kellogg, Steven. *Can I Keep Him?* Dial, 1971. A perfect story for all those children who cannot have a pet in their homes.

Potter, Beatrix. *The Tale of Peter Rabbit.* Warne, (n.d.) The breathtaking adventure tale of a disobedient rabbit named Peter.

Rey, H. A. *Curious George.* Houghton, 1941. The rib-tickling adventures of a monkey whose curiosity creates major disasters.

Viorst, Judith. *Alexander and the Terrible, Horrible, No Good, Very Bad Day*; il. by Ray Cruz. Atheneum, 1972. A perfect book for those very special days when only laughter can finally set things right.

Williams, Barbara. *Albert's Toothache*; il. by Kay Chorao. Dutton, 1974. The story of a misplaced toothache and a grandmother who knows where it really hurts.

Zion, Gene. *No Roses for Harry!* il. by Margaret Bly Graham. Harper, 1958. More adventures for Harry the dog, who hates to take baths and sweaters with roses.

Bibliography of Children's Books

Agostinelli, Maria Enrica. *I Know Something You Don't Know*; il. by the author. New York: Macmillan, 1971.

Ahlberg, Jane and Allan. *Each Peach Pear Plum*: il. by the authors. New York: Viking, 1978.

Barrett, Judi. *Animals Should Definitely Not Act Like People*; il. by Ron Barrett. New York: Atheneum, 1980.

Bester, Roger. *Guess What?* il. by the author. New York: Crown, 1980.

Briggs, Raymond. *The Snowman*; il. by the author. New York: Random, 1978.

Brody, Selma Rich. *Be-a-Train.* Miller-Brody Productions, Record or cassette with 12 activity books and teacher's guide. Random School Division, Dept. 288 A, 400 Hahn Road, Westminster, MD 21157.

DeRegniers, Beatrice Schenk. *May I Bring a Friend?* il. by Beni Montresor. New York: Atheneum, 1964.

Domanska, Janina. *What Do You See?* il. by the author. New York: Macmillan, 1974.

Emberley, Barbara. *Simon's Song*; adap. and il. by Ed Emberley. New York: Prentice-Hall, Inc., 1969.

Flack, Marjorie. *Ask Mr. Bear*; il. by the author. New York: Macmillan, 1932.

Françoise, pseud. (Françoise Seignobosc). *Jeanne-Marie Counts Her Sheep*; il. by the author. New York: Scribner, 1957.

Gág, Wanda. *Millions of Cats*; il. by the author. New York: Coward-McCann, 1928.

Galdone, Paul. *The Three Bears*; il. by the author. New York, Seabury, 1972.

———. *The Three Billy Goats Gruff*; il. by the author. New York: Seabury, 1973.

Ginsburg, Mirra. *Good Morning, Chick*; il. by Byron Barton. New York: Greenwillow, 1980.

Hoban, Tana. *Is It Red? Is It Yellow? Is It Blue?* il. by the author. New York: Greenwillow, 1978.

———. *Look Again!* il. by the author. New York: Macmillan, 1971.

Hogrogian, Nonny. *Apples*; il. by the author. New York: Macmillan, 1972.

Hush Little Baby, A Folk Lullaby; il. by Aliki Brandenberg. Englewood Cliffs, N.J.: Prentice-Hall, Inc., n.d.

Hutchins, Pat. *Changes, Changes*; il. by the author. New York: Macmillan, 1971.

———. *Rosie's Walk*; il. by the author. New York: Macmillan, 1968.

Kalan, Robert, *Rain*; il. by Donald Crews. New York: Greenwillow, 1978.

Langstaff, John. *Over in the Meadow*; il. by Feodor Rojankovsky. New York: Harcourt, 1957.

Maestro, Betsey. *Harriet Reads Signs and More Signs*; il. by Guilio Maestro. New York: Crown, 1981.

Panek, Dennis. *Detective Whoo*; il. by the author. New York: Bradbury, 1981.

Quackenbush, Robert. *Go Tell Aunt Rhody*; il. by the author. New York: Macmillan, 1968.

Rockwell, Anne. *Honk Honk!* il. by the author. New York: Dutton, 1980.

Scarry, Richard. *Lowly Worm Word Book*; il. by the author. New York: Random, 1981.

Seuss, Dr. pseud. (Theodor Geisel). *I Can Read With My Eyes Shut!* il. by the author. New York: Random, 1978.

Shiefman, Vicky. *M Is for Move*; il. by Bill Miller. New York: Elsevier-Dutton, 1981.

Stadler, John. *Cat at Bat*; il. by the author. New York: Dutton, 1979.

Turkle, Brinton. *Deep in the Forest*; il. by the author. New York: Dutton, 1976.

Ungerer, Tomi. *One, Two, Where's My Shoe?* il. by the author. New York: Harper, 1964.

————. *Snail, Where Are You?* il. by the author. New York. Harper, 1962.

Watanabe, Shigeo. *Get Set! Go!* il. by Yasuo Ohtomo. New York: Collins, 1980.

————. *What a Good Lunch!* il. by Yasuo Ohtomo. New York: Collins, 1980.

Wells, Rosemary. *Max's First Word*; il. by the author. New York: Dial, 1979.

————. *Max's New Suit*; il. by the author. New York: Dial, 1979.

————. *Max's Ride*; il. by the author. New York: Dial, 1979.

Wheeler, Cindy. *A Good Day, A Good Night*; il. by the author. New York: Lippincott, 1980.

Zacharias, Thomas. *But Where Is the Green Parrot?* il. by Wanda Zacharias. New York: Delacorte, 1968.

3

Reading at the First Grade Level (The Reader Grows Wings)

The formal reading process begins with the first grade. It is in the first grade that children begin the developmental reading program. A reading program is developmental in the sense that it has set systematic reading goals which an individual learner can be expected to achieve at a certain grade level. The program is, furthermore, developmental in that it takes each student through all the prescribed reading skills in an orderly fashion. The ultimate goal of any developmental reading program is to train students to become proficient lifetime readers.

Developmental reading programs do not necessarily take a single specific reading approach. The goals of the developmental reading program may be achieved through the use of either a basal reader approach, a language experience approach, an individualized approach, or an eclectic approach.

The Basal Reader Approach: An Overview of Materials and Terms

Although any of the approaches just mentioned might be applied in teaching reading at the first grade level, the basal reader approach is most frequently used in elementary schools throughout the United States. The basal reader approach is preferred because it is based on a set of standardized materials, commercially prepared, which help the reader to get from point A to point B in an orderly fashion. The basal reader approach does have some drawbacks; these will be described in the ensuing discussions.

Scope and Sequence: The Master Plan

In each basal program, a master plan, which the textbook companies refer to as "scope and sequence," guides the teacher and students through the program. The term *scope* defines the skills which are to be taught at a given grade level. It also defines in what depth each particular skill is to be taught. *Sequence* outlines which skills are to be taught at what specific grade level. The scope and sequence plan is usually included as part of the teacher edition of each basal reader. Many companies also print out a separate scope and sequence chart which can be very useful to both the teacher and the school library media specialist in determining what skills are taught at a certain grade level.

The basal reader approach to reading is based on the development of the following distinct categories of reading skills: word attack skills (also called decoding skills), comprehension skills (also called comprehension/literary skills), language skills, and study skills.

Word Attack (Decoding) Skills

Under the category of word attack skills (decoding skills) the reader learns to read using the following decoding methods: phonic analysis, structural analysis, picture clues, configuration, context clues, dictionary skills, and sight words (called high frequency words in 1980s basals).

Phonic analysis. When children decode words using the phonic analysis method they are expected to associate sounds (phonemes) with letters (graphemes). Learning to associate sounds with certain letters and letter combinations is essentially what reading is all about. It is, therefore, very important that children become skillful in letter-sound associations, for only then will they be able to participate in phonic analysis. Although phonic analysis is a most important skill which all children should master, not all children learn to read using only phonic analysis. In fact, many children apply various word attack skills in their reading efforts. At the first grade level, children frequently combine the sight word method, also called whole word method, with phonic analysis.

Structural analysis. The more advanced first grade reader may add another skill such as structural analysis to decode an unfamiliar word. When children are using structural analysis they are essentially dissecting words. They are, for instance, looking for compound words within words, or prefixes, suffixes, and inflectional endings.

Picture clues and configuration. At this grade level children are also encouraged to use picture clues to help unravel the meaning of unfamiliar words. Those children who have extreme difficulty with sound-letter (phoneme-grapheme) relationships are sometimes encouraged to see relationships between letter and object. This skill also may be termed "looking for configuration." A beautiful little picture book called the *Alphabeast Book*, written and illustrated by Dorothy Schmiderer,[1] demonstrates the configuration skill to perfection.

Context clues. Using context clues is another word attack skill which young readers must learn to use to the optimum. More advanced readers are also encouraged to use dictionary skills to "attack" words that are not familiar to them.

Comprehension Skills

Comprehension skills are also taught at the first grade level, and acquiring these skills in reading is as important as learning word attack skills. Readers must not only be able to decode words, they must also understand what the meaning is of the word which they have decoded. Recent studies which investigated the reading abilities of elementary school children throughout the United States have indicated that although children were making progress in their reading abilities, they were still falling short in their abilities to comprehend the material they were reading.

Comprehension skills are usually categorized into the following areas: literal comprehension, interpretive comprehension, critical reading, and creative reading.

Literal comprehension. The easiest comprehension skill for readers in the first grade to learn is literal comprehension. It requires that readers acquire the ability to search for specific information within the material they are reading. First grade children, for example, might be asked to give the name of the characters in the story. Literal comprehension is also applied when the reader is asked to follow specific directions. Examples are the ability to follow directions to assemble an object or to prepare a recipe. Literal comprehension may be taught either during an oral reading lesson or during a reading lesson that requires the student to complete a workbook page.

Interpretive comprehension. At the first grade level, this is already a far more difficult skill to learn for it asks that readers begin to read "between" the lines to state cause and effect or to detect a specific mood which the author wanted to present. First grade teachers usually help children learn this skill through oral discussion, during which individual children are asked, "What would you have done?" "Why would you . . . ?" or "How would you . . . ?" Interpretive comprehension is also taught using the pictures that accompany the story to clarify cause and effect relationships or the mood of the story, which only may have been implied in the text.

Interpretive comprehension also includes the skill of being able to select and state the main idea of a selection. Searching for the main idea is a somewhat difficult task for first graders since it demands that readers select correctly from various possibilities. Interpretive comprehension is taught through oral discussion or through the use of workbooks in which students have to select the correct answer from several choices.

Critical reading. This is another skill taught under the category of comprehension. The skill requires that readers begin to evaluate material in order to tell whether the author has used fact or opinion. Although some first graders are already able to apply some critical reading skills and can state rather specifically whether a selection is fact or fiction or fact or opinion, most are not able to apply this skill until they become more fluent in their reading.

Creative reading. The highest comprehension skill that first grade children will have to master is that of creative reading. It is a skill requiring that students read with imagination and apply this imagination to the material they are reading. This means readers have acquired the ability to understand cause and effect relationships and apply this knowledge to explain why characters in a story behave the way they do, even though the author has not supplied all the details. Reading creatively also means being able to make value judgments and to predict the outcomes of stories. It can also mean that readers have both the ability and the desire to use the reading materials to solve some of their own personal problems.

First grade children who are able to comprehend their reading materials at the creative level usually try to share with the teacher and other students how they feel about a story and how they feel about the behavior of the characters. Some children also try to tell willing listeners how the story might apply to their lives. Children who read creatively are also far more eager to point out their dissatisfaction with stories that have trite plots or lack imaginative story lines. First graders, in their unabashed ways, will usually refer to such reading materials as "dumb" stories. Creative readers, in particular, have to be watched with great care so that they do not become reluctant readers because of reading materials that fail to challenge their talents.

Language Skills

Language skills are also included in the first grade reading program to help the learner recognize that printed words are like oral language written down. Under the category of language skills the learner is taught the necessity for punctuation marks; the use of capitalization; the various parts of a sentence, as well as syntax; the use of idiomatic expressions and hyperboles; the use of synonyms, homographs, and homonyms. The various language skills are introduced and reinforced at various learning stages to insure that students become very well versed in this particular area.

Study Skills

Study skills help students, including first graders, to become efficient readers and learners. Many of the study skills could just as well be called library media center skills. For instance, the study skill of recognizing the various parts of a book, including its author and illustrator, is a skill basic to understanding the use of the card catalog and the overall arrangement of the school library media center. Likewise, the study skill of alphabetizing is another skill that is necessary for the use of the card catalog. The study skills involved in using maps and globes and interpreting graphs, tables, and charts likewise could be called library media center skills, since these really are reference skills. Study skills that cover the use of encyclopedias, almanacs, gazetteers, and yearbooks may also be referred to as library media center skills. In fact, many basal publishers do refer to these as an area of library media center skills or simply library skills. The arrangement of the school library media center and the arrangement of the catalog are definitely skills that should be labeled more specifically as library media center skills. Thus, study skills and library media center skills are closely related.

Looking in on a Basal Reader Lesson

Teaching a reading lesson to twenty or thirty first graders is not an easy task. It is more like a miracle that a teacher can take a group of youngsters of various learning abilities, cultural backgrounds, and states of emotional, physical, and intellectual development and within ten months get them to read at least several hundred words.

The process of getting a group of six- and seven-year-olds to read might be considered an even greater challenge if one considers that many schools do not allow more than one to two hours per day, at most, to the teaching of reading. Although reading does take place in other subject areas as well—in mathematics, social studies, and science—the formal teaching of reading as a subject is limited to an inordinately brief period of time.

The scarcity of time is particularly noticeable when teachers divide their children into reading groups, a common practice. For example, a class of twenty-four children is usually divided into three reading groups. With an hour and a half set aside for reading, the teacher has thirty minutes to work with each reading group. Thirty minutes in itself seems like a fair amount of time for teaching reading to children of this age. Of course the time shrinks quickly when the thirty minutes are divided by eight, so that the actual time allotted is less than four minutes per child. Even when two hours are set aside for reading, each child is allowed less than five minutes. Then too, it must be remembered that in gathering a group some time is lost in settling children down. It does take time for children to leave their desks, search for their reading materials, find their pencils, get to the area set aside for reading, and, finally, settle in their assigned seats. Even with the best disciplined group, precious minutes are lost. During the lesson, the teacher, while working with one group, still has to oversee the other sixteen children who are now left on their own at their desks. Especially in classrooms where children have not reached the maturity level to work on their own without constant teacher supervision, time is lost because the teacher must stop the reading lesson frequently to guide and discipline the other children, who are supposed to be working quietly.

Because of the time limitation and other problems associated with grouping, some classroom teachers are electing to teach reading to the entire class at one time. The additional time, gained through this method, is then used to help children who need special attention.

The Five-Step Basal Reader Lesson

Since time is of the greatest importance when teaching reading, each lesson must be introduced in an orderly fashion. This structured process, referred to as the DRA (directed reading activity), includes the following reading steps: preparation for reading, silent reading, oral reading, follow-up activities, and extension activities. The DRA strategy is not limited to the basal reader lesson; it may also be used when teaching reading with the language experience or individualized approach.

Step 1: Preparation. Preparation for reading means the teacher prepares students for the reading material which will be covered during a particular day. During preparation, many teachers try to personalize the reading materials by asking questions that will fit the needs of the individual reader. In using this teaching technique, teachers hope to develop in the reader greater interest and enthusiasm for the materials to be covered. During preparation, new words that will be used in the story to be read are introduced.

At the first grade level teachers rely heavily on the phonetic method, sight word method, picture clue method, and context clue method to help children to decode new words. As students progress in reading, other word attack skills, such as structural analysis and dictionary skills, are added.

Step 2: Silent reading. Silent reading is exactly what the term means: the student reads a portion of the basal reader silently without the help of the teacher. However, a well-planned silent reading period is begun with carefully prepared instructions which the student must follow in order to achieve certain objectives. For example, teachers usually instruct students to apply certain word attack skills to decode unfamiliar words. Students are usually instructed also to apply comprehension skills so that they will be able to answer questions relating to their reading after they have finished their silent reading. Students in first grade usually do not spend much time on the silent reading portion of a reading lesson until they have acquired some basic independent reading abilities. At the beginning of the year silent reading and oral reading are usually taught concurrently. The teacher might instruct students to read one paragraph orally and then immediately pose questions which the students must answer by reading the text silently to find the answers.

Step 3: Oral reading. First grade students usually spend a major portion of their reading lesson on oral reading. During oral reading, teachers check how competently students use the all-important word attack skills to read their assigned stories. At the same time, teachers also check how efficiently students read. The reading process itself requires that the reader move from word to word and line to line in saccadic or rhythmic movements. In other words, the eyes of the reader move and stop, move and stop. The stops that the reader makes are called fixations. What a reader perceives during a fixation is referred to as a perception span. Beginning readers have far more fixations and a far more limited perception span than experienced readers. Part of the oral reading process is, therefore, used to help inexperienced readers develop their perception span and decrease the number of fixations they make during reading.

Teachers also help children develop their enunciation, pronunciation, and overall reading fluency during oral reading. Children are also alerted during oral reading to the punctuation marks, so that the voice inflection called for by punctuation marks may be developed.

Diagnosing Reading Problems during an Oral Reading Lesson

Even though children are screened for vision and hearing problems before they enter first grade, some children still enter first grade with such problems undiagnosed. During oral reading, teachers can quickly observe whether children have visual, hearing, or other problems that might hinder their reading performance. Some of the telltale signs of vision problems are squinting, holding the book too close, holding a hand over the eye, or red and inflamed eyes. Children who continually lose their place during a reading lesson also may have vision problems. Inattentiveness by children when the teacher works at the chalkboard may be another indicator that they cannot focus on the words the teacher is writing.

Hearing loss can sometimes be detected when children are inattentive, constantly ask that instructions be repeated, complain of frequent earaches, or show signs of dizziness. Although not all reading problems are related to the symptoms just described, teachers who notice that particular students have great difficulty in reading usually check for vision and hearing loss.

Oral reading also helps teachers to detect speech problems. For first graders who have lost their front teeth, this may be only a temporary problem. However, students who have a stuttering problem might be temporarily excused from oral reading until they have worked with a speech therapist who will then make recommendations as to classroom procedures.

Reading problems which might be attributed to dyslexia also are usually noted during oral reading lessons. The most obvious problems would be the reader's attempt to read from right to left and to reverse letters and words.

Oral reading practices can be very enjoyable experiences for most children. They can, however, be very traumatic for children who have vision, hearing, or speech problems. Oral reading can be even more traumatic for children who are extremely shy and withdrawn and who simply are not ready to perform when placed among a group of children. Careful attention must be paid to these children who display one or more of the described symptoms so that they will not become disabled or reluctant readers so early in their reading careers.

Step 4: Follow-up activities. After silent and oral reading have been completed, the reading lesson moves on to follow-up activities. These activities aim at reinforcing skills to which students have been introduced during the silent or oral portion of their reading lesson. Follow-up activities in most cases involve students in completing workbook exercises. Students may also be asked to listen to a tape, record, or record/filmstrip. The audiovisual item may be synchronized with a worksheet or a special supplementary reader.

The use of audiovisual materials in teaching reading can be very beneficial if they allow the reader to interact with them. For instance, high frequency words (sight words) can be reinforced if the reader can supply the words during the playing of the tape. Tapes and records may also be used to help students become more fluent readers by demonstrating to them how the story should be read. Filmstrips can be a very helpful tool when they introduce and reinforce reading study skills, such as how to use the card catalog, or how to use the encyclopedia.

Only when follow-up activities are carefully introduced by the teacher will students achieve the expected reading goals. This guidance is especially needed for workbook lessons because even updated versions of basal reader workbooks have not succeeded at providing instructions simple enough for first and second graders to comprehend and follow. Even if children can read the instructions, they may not be able to interpret the illustrations which they must use in order to complete the work sheet. For example, an illustration of "snorkle" in one workbook looked more like a safety pin. Snorkle, the gear used for diving, would in itself be a rather obscure object for many children; if so, it is very unlikely that they could relate to the "sn" they were supposed to fill in before "orkle." The same exercise also asked children to look at another picture that looked more like two Christmas tree ornaments than the snowflakes the students would have to name in order to supply the "sn." Students who are unable to read and follow the instructions or decipher pictures will not be able to complete some of the follow-up activities successfully. Students who do not have the emotional maturity to work independently will also be unable to complete the follow-up activities with any measure of success. The point that must be emphasized again is that this component of the basal lesson will be successful only if the teacher is able to devote enough time to explain the materials in detail.

Step 5: Extension activities. The final component of the reading lesson is referred to as extension activities, sometimes called enrichment activities. Extension activities are planned to show young readers that reading does not stop with the basal reader but rather extends far beyond the basal reader to books and other materials, which can be read for pleasure and information. Extension activities might also be rightly called fulfillment activities in that they fulfill the need of individual readers to read as much or as little as they wish.

Classroom teachers usually allow for extension activities by setting up a reading corner in the classroom. Many classroom teachers also work with library media specialists in selecting and developing special reading lists from which individual readers may select their books for extension activity reading. The reading corner will be discussed further in chapter 6. Extension activities may also take the form of creative endeavors, such as dramatization of the reading materials through the use of puppets. They may also involve the use of nonprint media such as filmstrips, tapes, and cassettes. Extension activities are limited only by time, materials, and each teacher's own creative imagination.

Pros and Cons of the Basal Reader Approach

The basal reader approach to reading is a very acceptable approach to reading for first graders. The carefully planned and structured materials are both teacher and student oriented. In some cases materials are even parent oriented and include special letters in both English and Spanish which can be forwarded to parents to keep them up to date on the progress of their children.

The program is teacher oriented in that instructors are provided with a "teacher edition," which carefully outlines how specific skills might be taught. The teacher edition suggests lead questions to help teachers in developing questioning techniques appropriate for the learners. Experienced teachers, of course, may not need all the guidelines provided, and some teachers even object to all the suggestions because they tend to stifle their own creativity. However, new teachers find the suggestions most helpful and reassuring in planning reading lessons to address the skills that have to be taught at a certain grade level.

The basal reader approach to reading also provides a measure of uniformity and continuity from grade level to grade level within a school or within an entire school district. Most basal reader publishers provide pretests, post-tests, and unit tests so that the school system can constantly monitor the progress that its students are making. In an age of accountability, this is a distinct advantage for administrators who might have to jutsify reading scores to parents. Supplementary materials, such as tapes, recordings, filmstrips, and workbooks are also welcomed by school districts which have to provide various learning modes for children of different cultural, language, and experiential backgrounds.   .

The more recent basals reflect a dramatic change in reading

instruction at the first grade level. During the 1950s much of the reading instruction centered around the sight word approach. This meant that children were only taught a certain number of sight words at a time. The sight words were reinforced repeatedly in a number of stories until mastery was assured. In a 1967 book, Jean Chall argued, on the basis of a survey of methods used between 1910 and 1965 for teaching children to read, that beginning readers could indeed learn to read using the phonics method, what Chall called code emphasis.[2] Basals published in the 1970s and 1980s reflect Chall's approach to teaching reading; most suggest an immediate letter-sound approach (phonic approach) to reading at the first grade level. The term "sight word" or "whole word" has virtually disappeared from the 1980 basals but has been replaced with the term "high frequency word." High frequency words such as *and, can, dog, down, go, he, I, no, out, up, yes*, and *you* are words which a child should know well, or, in all honesty, know "on sight." However, basal companies recommend that children may also learn these words using the phonic analysis and context clue decoding methods. It is anticipated, of course, that once children have acquired the ability to decode words using various decoding methods they may expand their word knowledge more rapidly than through the former sight word memorization method. This in itself might help children overcome some of the problems they formerly encountered when changing from one basal series to another.

Despite the advantages, there are also some serious drawbacks to basal reader programs. Their most serious drawback is that they tempt teachers to rely too much on basal readers. When students are not allowed to read books and other reading materials of their own choice because the basal reader takes precedence, the basal reader could turn out to be very detrimental; preventing children from becoming familiar with the real world of reading that is waiting for them. Basal readers should never be used other than as tools to open the doors to the wider world of reading.

Another serious drawback is the overall makeup of reading material in the basal reader. Because of the large investment that a textbook company makes in developing a basal reader series, it must try to sell its product to as many schools as possible. Because the publisher needs to reach the largest market possible, the content of the readers must be developed to be attractive to as many people as possible. Thus, the development of a body of stories that will appeal to city and country children, as well as to children from the various minority groups found within each school, is a task which simply is not accomplished to the satisfaction of all concerned. Someone, somewhere, somehow does not fit into the general scheme of any given basal reader. Whenever this is the case, alternatives must be provided.

Similarly, basal reader texts are somewhat restricted, reaching neither the more talented reader nor the reader who performs below the required norm. Although many companies suggest enrichment activities for either group, the fact remains that basal readers are written essentially to reach the average student. The term "average," however, is not interpreted consistently among the various basal publishers. This is particularly evidenced by the wide diversity of the numbers and types of words introduced at each grade level by the different basal publishers. A research study that compared the first grade basal readers of the 1960s with those published in 1970 indicated that the number of words introduced in 1970 first grade readers ranged from 324 to 675. In the 1960s the vocabulary had ranged only from 235 to 354 words. The increase in vocabulary from the 1960s to 1970 ranged from 89 words for one publisher to 340 words for another. The study, furthermore, pointed out that the Harcourt Brace and Macmillan first grade programs had only 248 and 235 words, respectively, in common with the 675-word Scott-Foresman basal for first grade.[3] A perusal of the basal readers published in 1980 and 1981 reveals that very similar problems still exist.

In summary, it might be said that the effectiveness of a basal reader approach to reading depends on the quality of the basal reader series, the manner in which the teacher uses the basal reader with students, and, ultimately, how students relate to the basal reader.

The Language Experience Approach to Reading

The language experience approach to reading is probably the second most widely used reading approach in the first grade. Schools with many children whose English-speaking abilities are limited use it most widely. It is also favored in schools with a large enrollment of children who have a limited reading readiness background and exhibit poor language development. The rationale of the language experience approach was proposed by Roach Van Allen in the 1960s, who suggested that if children can hear a word, they can speak it; if they can speak it, they can either write it down, or someone can write it down for them; if they can write it, they also want to and can read the material they have written. What all of this means is that teacher and students essentially create their own readers.

The Language Experience Approach in Action

To get the reading lesson started when using language experience approach, teachers usually bring unique objects or special picture books to share with their children. Objects or books are selected for their sensory appeal so that students can explore them by touching, listening, or even tasting. Food, in fact, is popular because it lends itself to wide-ranging sensory explorations and lively follow-up discussions. Books that explore basic concepts such as sounds, colors, and shapes are also very popular because they encourage the reader to use specific senses during participation. Teachers usually initiate the lesson by asking many "why," "how," and "what" questions.

After ample time has been devoted to looking and talking about the object or book, the teacher moves on to the more formal aspect of the lesson by asking each student to talk about the object in one complete sentence. Children with very limited oral language skills are usually helped along by the teacher, who might give the child a partial sentence, which is then completed by the child. For example, "The pizza tasted _____." The sentences provided by the students are recorded by the teacher on a large piece of paper, called the language experience chart. This chart, in essence, becomes the basal reader, because children learn to read using the words and sentences recorded on the chart. Teachers, therefore, try to structure the discussions in such a manner that the sentences provided by students develop into something like a story. This story is then used for oral reading practice. The stories created by the children are also used for teaching and practicing decoding skills and comprehension skills.

Many of the stories written by the teacher and children are duplicated for children to take home and share with their parents. The stories are also collected in special reading folders that are kept for each child. As the year progresses, students are given more and more responsibility for talking and writing about objects brought to class by the teacher and students. Special planned field trips or guest speakers in the classroom also provide avenues of creativity.

The success of the language experience approach to reading depends very much on the teacher's skill and experience at teaching reading. The approach is very time consuming and very demanding, because the teacher is solely responsible for planning a reading program that covers all the word attack and comprehension skills necessary for a particular grade. The teacher must also be able to create an environment in which children grow in their learning abilities through creative activities that suit the learning modalities of each individual. The teacher must have a very creative and organized mind in order to keep the learning process moving ahead on an even keel.

The language experience approach to reading is usually phased out at the end of the first grade or at the beginning of the second grade, whenever children have acquired language skills and reading attitudes that will make it possible for them to function in a classroom using either the standard basal text or other reading materials.

The Individualized Approach to Reading

The individualized approach to reading is rarely used at the first grade level since the approach requires that children have the maturity and basic reading skills to read on their own with only periodic instruction by the teacher. If it is used at all in the first grade, it is used with children who exceed the usual first grader in reading ability. The approach is more commonly used at the intermediate grades, so the discussion of this approach will be included in chapter 7.

The Eclectic Approach to Reading or "Mulligan Stew"

An eclectic approach to reading is used in many first grade classrooms. It is gaining in popularity because it allows teachers to use the teaching methods of the basal reader approach, the language experience approach, and the individualized approach. The eclectic approach to reading might best be described as the "mulligan stew" approach: the choicest ingredients of any reading approach are used to help children become successful readers.

Notes

1. Dorothy Schmiderer, *Alphabeast Book: An Abecedarium*; il. by the author (New York: Holt, 1971).

2. Jeanne S. Chall, *Learning to Read: The Great Debate* (New York: McGraw-Hill, 1967), p. 307.

3. Leo V. Rodenborn and Earlene Washburn, "Some Implications of the New Basal Reader," *Elementary English* 51:885–87 (Sept. 1974).

4

Role of the School Library Media Specialist in the First Grade Reading Program

School library media specialists can play a vital role in the first grade reading program. Their sphere of influence extends not only to the classroom and its teachers and students but also includes cooperative efforts involving the building principal, the reading supervisor, and the remedial reading teacher.

In becoming part of the teaching team, school library media specialists have many opportunities to share their wide-ranging professional expertise as master teachers, storytellers, and experts in material selection. As master teachers in team teaching situations, they demonstrate new teaching ideas, which can be carried out in the classroom or library media center. As master storytellers, enthusiastic story readers, and book reviewers, they lead children toward the wonderful discovery that learning to read opens up worlds of reading adventures which will become even more exciting as their reading abilities increase. As experts in materials selection, they can offer valuable information to classroom teachers, remedial reading teachers, reading supervisors, and principals on how to select materials both to complement the reading goals of the school and to meet the reading needs of individual students.

The Need to be Members of the Teaching Team

The success of a reading program depends very much on how closely school library media specialists become involved with the classroom reading activities. Many school library media specialists and administrators probably feel that their library media center programs are already very much involved if children can come to check out materials, either on regular scheduled classroom visits or in an open library media center arrangement. This certainly is an acceptable way of becoming involved with the reading program, at least as a first step.

However, the weekly visit or open library media center concept arrangement can become even more beneficial for both teachers and students if library media specialists and teachers can plan some activities that tie in directly with the lessons presently taught in the classroom. For example, first graders who are introduced to the concept of alphabetizing in their basal readers can be told by the library media specialist that the card catalog is arranged in the same alphabetical order. They might also be shown that the library media center's picture books are arranged in the same manner. Each child might even be given a picture book and asked to find the shelf which would correspond to the appropriate letter of the alphabet.

Teachers and school library media specialists can also cooperate in teaching and reinforcing lessons which acquaint students with the various literary genres introduced in their basal readers. For instance, a folktale which might have been introduced in an abbreviated version in the reader may be read by the library media specialist in its original version the next time the children visit the library. The library media specialist may even wish to take the opportunity to share with children the different illustrative techniques used by different artists to illustrate the same tale. In planning reading lessons cooperatively teachers and library media specialists can enrich and satisfy each individual student's reading needs to the fullest potential.

How to Become a Member of the Teaching Team

School library media specialists who wish to tie their library media center programs directly into the reading program will have to be the initiators. They should take their plans of action directly to the reading supervisor, curriculum supervisor, and building principal.

How enthusiastically the school library media specialist is received by these administrators depends largely on how, when, and where the plans are presented. Plans presented to administrators during brief informal conversations in the hallway rarely get off the ground, and, if they do, they will in all likelihood not receive the educational recompense they deserve. School library media specialists should, therefore, schedule a formal meeting with each administrator so that they can present their plans of action, for which they will later be held accountable. The plan itself might be developed using the general outline that follows.

The library media specialist and reading teachers will meet at least once during the school year, a separate meeting being held for each grade level. Each meeting will consider:
1. How to prepare one cooperative reading/library media center lesson per month per grade level
2. Other cooperation between basal reader lessons and media center lessons (Some ideas will appear later in this chapter.)
3. Modifications of these plans
4. A basic instrument to measure effectiveness of programs

When meeting the principal, the school library media specialist should ask the principal's help in scheduling the proposed meetings with the teachers. The announcement that meetings will take place should come from the principal and might be announced during a regular faculty meeting. Library media specialists might even wish to suggest that they be allowed at the faculty meeting to elaborate briefly on the plans after the principal has made the general announcement. This elaboration would simply consist of outlining very briefly what specific steps the library media specialist proposes to take to enrich the school's basal reader program. (Although one might wish really to use the term "improve" rather than "enrich," a more modest stance will help win the confidence of teachers, who do not need another "I know better than you" program, but might be receptive to an "I want to be involved" program.)

Becoming a Member of the Basal Reader Selection Committee

The library media specialist also should become a member of the basal reader selection committee, so that the school can take full advantage of this professional's expertise in material selection. To become a member of this committee, the library media specialist needs to step forward and offer her or his services.

This may seem at first glance to be yet another time-consuming task for school library media specialists who already have very demanding schedules. When the time comes to select a basal series, many hours will have to be devoted to reviewing basals individually and in group meetings. However, basal readers are not selected annually; this is usually done every five to eight years. The contributions of school library media specialists to their selection are many and important. By virtue of their professional training they can quickly detect whether a basal series is truly interested in furthering lifetime reading habits in its users.

A good basal series lists outstanding supplementary reading on diverse subjects, including books which not only meet standards of excellence but also are readily available in established school library media center collections. Who better than the library media specialist will be able to determine whether a given basal series complements the holdings of the school library media center? Finally, participation in the selection of a basal series gives the school library media specialist the opportunity to promote basals that teach library media center skills and study skills through the reading program and which may also be applied continuously through the use of the school library media center.

Selecting the Basal Reader

The school library media specialist who is on the basal reader selection committee should focus her or his attention on those aspects of the basal relevant to making students interested and lifelong readers. Teachers' expertise will be focused more on how well the basal program will work in the classroom. The discussion that follows will concern mostly those areas in which the library media specialist has expertise, but they should consult some of the following professional review sources for general information: *Guidelines for Selecting Bias-Free Textbooks and Storybooks*,[1] *Handbook for Evaluating and Selecting Curriculum Materials*,[2] and the reviews of individual basal readers in *The Reading Teacher, Language Arts,* and *Curriculum Review,* which may be located through the use of *Education Index.*

In approaching the various aspects of evaluating a basal reader series school library media specialists need to follow certain criteria to justify their critiques. To evaluate the basal reader series for story content the evaluation might be based on the same criteria used for selecting literature for the general library media center collection. The questions asked would include some of the following:

1. Is there a good balance between the various genres of literature? For instance, are there stories of modern fantasy as well as traditional folktales and fables? Are there stories of contemporary fiction as well as historical fiction? Are there samples of current biography as well as historical biography? Does the series include poetry which will make

the reader laugh as well as contemplate? Are there stories which will inform students and encourage them to pursue their own inquiries?

2. Do the various literary genres represented in the series meet the standards of excellence in plot, theme, characterization, setting, style, and format?

3. Have various ethnic groups and cultural minorities been represented honestly and without prejudice?

4. Are the stories free of stereotyping?

5. Do the stories contain a generous amount of humor?

6. Do the illustrations have artistic quality and appropriate details to provide the reader with picture clues? (Since readers will use picture clues to help their reading efforts, pictures should complement and enhance the story.)

Library media specialists definitely need to find out how many of the stories used in the readers are already on the library shelves and how many are still available for purchase. This consideration is crucial because one of the most important yet neglected aspects of reading is the component that shows students that the story excerpt in the basal reader can be read in its entirety in a book. Many teachers build up tremendous excitement about a basal story only to see that excitement vanish when students discover that they will never find out how the story ends. The interest which students initially show could, however, be maintained and strengthened if teachers and school library media specialists would cooperate and demonstrate to eager students that the stories can be found in books in the library.

Basal reader publishers who are concerned with the development of lifetime reading habits in students usually include an "enrichment" or "additional reading" selection of books, which can be useful for both teacher and students. Some publishers also provide bibliographies which categorize additional reading suggestions according to reading abilities. In a few instances publishers provide bibliographies that make suggestions to the teacher for read-aloud stories.

Some publishers of basal readers also furnish separate supplementary reading bibliographies. These are usually arranged according to grade level and match the content of the basal reader for that grade. School library media specialists will find the bibliographies invaluable in planning reading programs, in checking library holdings, and in ordering books for their collection. Bibliographies may be requested from the publishers by contacting their regional or home offices.

Finally, school library media specialists must evaluate how well basal readers have covered the all-encompassing areas of study skills and library media center skills. Basal readers need to be carefully examined to determine how these skills have been introduced within the overall scope and sequence of the reading program. Library media specialists need to review what recommendations have been made to the teachers as to how these skills can be accomplished. The question that needs to be asked is, "Does the basal reader suggest that the school library media center be used to complement and reinforce study skills and library media center skills or are they mainly reinforced only through workbook pages?"

Skills that are designated as study skills are in many instances really skills which can be taught far more effectively in the school library media center through the cooperation of library media specialist and teacher. The former, being experts on how to evaluate and teach library media center skills, can quickly determine whether library media center skill lessons have been simply thrown in because they have to be taught at some point or have been carefully incorporated into specific lessons, which necessitate that certain library media center skills be developed in order that a reading goal may be achieved. Any basal series which completely overlooks to recommend that teachers and library media specialists cooperate in teaching these skills should be considered ineffective in guiding children towards becoming self-reliant lifetime library users.

Every School Library Media Center Needs a Set of Basal Readers

A complete set of the basal reader series which has been adopted for a particular school should be requested for and kept in the school library media center. This request seems too obvious to mention, yet this necessary practice has not been implemented in many schools. All too many elementary school library media specialists have no access to the basal readers used in their schools because too often administrators have overlooked the vital connection between the school library media center and the basal reader program.

Library media specialists need constant access to the basal readers so that they can plan reading activities that tie in directly with the reading lessons which are taking place in the classrooms. They are far too busy to have to take the time to search for or request the basal readers from the various teachers. The basal readers must be accessible in the school library media center at any time so that at a moment's notice teacher and library media specialist can look at the basal and make plans for reinforcement and enrichment lessons.

School library media specialists also need access to the basal readers so that they can search their contents for books or excerpts of books that are available for purchase in trade editions. This point was already made under basal reader selection; however, it needs to be reiterated in order to establish the real need of a set of basal readers for every school library media center. Basal readers also need to be examined carefully (that is, if the publisher does not provide a separate bibliography) for enrichment reading, also called additional reading, which is usually included at the end of each unit in the teacher's edition. All the books suggested under this category should be made readily available on the school library media center shelves.

Library media specialists also need access to the basal readers to enable them to check the thematic development within specific units. In many instances they can enrich a unit by suggesting to teachers additional print and nonprint materials which will help explain the subject of the unit in greater depth. These specialized materials will be welcomed by students with various interests as well as learning abilities.

Everyone concerned with the welfare of future readers must always remember that basal readers are limited in meeting the reading needs of each individual child. In fact, students who have been asked by teachers and parents why they read often have been unable to come up with answers which indicate they understand that knowing how to read is essential for survival in today's society. To remedy this sad state of affairs, students need to be exposed to more opportunities that show the relationship between the basal reader lesson and the real world of reading. This connection can only be made if library media specialist and teacher share in the responsibility of opening up the basal reader lesson to the abundance of supplementary materials available through the school library media center.

In conclusion, if there is need to present yet another reason why school library media specialists should have ready access to basal readers, the answer might be, "School library media specialists are also reading teachers and, as such, have a firsthand need for access to basal readers."

Ideas for Implementing the Teaching Role

The ideas that follow are based on one motto, "Reaching more children with books to open up the wider world of reading through the library." The ideas are, therefore, mainly book oriented. They are meant to serve as springboards for teachers and students, to encourage them to reach for more ambitious reading goals. Some ideas are more appropriate for whole class participation, while others reach out to the individual learner.

Most of the ideas can be carried out easily by the school library media specialist and do not require hours of preparation. Their simplicity should, however, not be looked upon as making them less effective in the teaching/learning arena. The simplicity of the ideas should, instead, be accepted as a special mark of distinction in that books, when carefully selected, will speak for themselves and do not need special trappings to catch the reader's attention. "Back to basics" should mean reaching more readers directly through books, rather than through peripheral, nonreading activities.

IDEA: Learning parts of the book. First graders are usually introduced to the various components that make up a book shortly after they have received their basal readers. Getting to know the terminology used to identify the various components of a book is of utmost importance to all children, because daily reading routines depend on children's ability to follow and interpret reading instructions such as, "Turn the page . . ."; "Who is the author?" "How can we find the story?" and "Locate the title of the story."

Many first grade children are quite overwhelmed by all these details and have great difficulty keeping up with the reading requirements. The library media specialist can, therefore, take some time either before or after a read-aloud session and reinforce the names we give to the parts of the book. Discussion of author, illustrator, and title can be easily incorporated in a read-aloud session by asking children to participate in identifying what the story is all about, who wrote the story, and how do we know?

Another approach to teaching the parts of the book is for the school library media specialist to construct a large "dummy" with the help of the children. The activity might be stretched out over several weeks. The content of the book should, if at all possible, include written work and drawings children have produced in their classrooms. Children who are not ready to undertake independent writing might be asked to submit their best workbook pages.

The various parts of a book can also be taught through the examination of proofs and galleys, which may be requested from children's book publishers. It may be suggested that an extra copy of the finished book be acquired so that it may be kept with the proofs and be available for examination at any time.

The highlight of any book discussion would, of course, be the appearance of a children's author who could share with children how books are created. Having a "real" author on hand would also show children that "real people" write books.

IDEA: Building reading skills through nursery rhymes and poetry. Early in the school year, many teachers begin to search for materials to make their reading skills lessons more enjoyable and meaningful. Within a few weeks, word attack skills lessons which in the beginning seemed to arouse eager participation by children become tiresome for many young readers who were weaned on the visual excitement of television. Instead of moving forward at a steady pace, the reading process is slowing down as children become apathetic with reading routines based mainly on workbook exercises. At this point school library media specialists can do much to inject new life into the teaching of reading skills by introducing children, when they visit the school library media center, to the world of nursery rhymes and poetry.

To teach a sense of sound, rhyme, and rhythm within words and word families, library media specialists might wish to open and close some library media center sessions with such favorite nursery rhymes as "Sing a Song of Sixpence," "Jack Be Nimble," "Hickory, Dickory, Dock," "One, Two, Buckle My Shoe," "Humpty Dumpty." One session might even be devoted to the special picture book version of "Old Mother Hubbard." After the rhymes have either been recited or read by the library media specialist, the children should then be encouraged to participate either individually or as a group in reciting the rhymes a second or even third time. In this manner children will develop a keener awareness of the sounds and rhyming qualities of words. A brief discussion of some of the rather unique words used in the rhymes will also help children to become more familiar with the alluring variety of language.

The school library media specialist may give the teacher a collection of nursery rhymes at the end of the read-aloud session so that the rhymes may be repeated in the classroom during the following days and weeks when phonics are taught and children experience difficulty with certain short and long vowel sounds.

Selecting poetry for first grade children can be both delightful and time consuming. It can be a delightful task because poetry can bring so much joy to the learning environment. It can also be a time consuming task because poems chosen for this grade level must be just right in both content and length to suit the young readers' temperaments. Poems selected must be childlike and contain figures of speech and literary allusions related to the more immediate world of the young listener.

Six- and seven-year-olds will delight in poems that tickle their funny bones and help them burst forth with hearty chuckles. They will also enjoy poetry that appeals to their senses and tickles their palate as well as their nose. Not to be overlooked for this age group are poems that will explain some of the anger, fear, and loneliness that children experience at home and school. Poems chosen for the first grade must take all of these requirements into consideration so that young readers will begin to experience the joy and satisfaction that can come through sharing this very special genre of literature.

Although school library media specialists usually have access to a fine basic poetry collection from which to select poems suitable for this grade level, additional suggestions may be gleaned from the first grade basal reader. Many of the first grade basal readers published within the last few years include poems by such well-known poets as Dorothy Aldis, Gwendolyn Brooks, Marchette Chute, Aileen Fisher, Karla Kuskin, David McCord, Mary O'Neill, Beatrice Schenk De Regniers, and Arnold Shapiro. Basal publishers seem unanimously to agree that poetry should be read aloud to children. Only after children have savored the experience of listening to poetry should they be asked to read it on their own. Basal publishers have opened the doors for poetry experiences. Library media specialists must now lead children and teachers through the doors towards even richer poetry experiences.

IDEA: Use read-aloud sessions to teach about the world of make-believe. Library media specialists have a superb opportunity to share the age-old and very rich world of fairy tales and fables with first graders, because these two genres are usually studied at this grade level. First graders are usually expected to develop certain basic literary skills in order to distinguish stories that are real from those that are called fairy tales or fanciful. ("Fanciful" is a more general term sometimes used to refer to this literary genre.) Children learn at this grade level that fairy tales take place in a world of make-believe, inhabited by people and animals with supernatural powers. Some basal readers also introduce students to the fact that many fairy tales follow certain patterns of writing and content. Such literary devices may be very obvious to an adult. However, for first graders, especially those who have not had many opportunities for listening to fairy tales, the skills are rather complex and can only be learned if teachers and library media specialists cooperate and reinforce the concepts over several weeks instead of the brief time that might be available during the regularly scheduled reading periods.

In planning read-aloud sessions to strengthen children's literary awareness, fairy tales should be selected that are either variants of those presented in the basal text or are similar to those in the basal in pattern (motif) or style. Variants of such familiar tales as "Cinderella," "Stone Soup," "Lazy Jack," "Tom Tit Tot," and "The Enormous Turnip" lend themselves very nicely to the discussion of literary components which children are directed to learn about. However, great care must be taken not to overdo the teaching part lest the read-aloud session turn into a teaching disaster by preventing any kind of independent thinking. Children in the library media center setting should be provided with open-ended questions rather than true or false ones, which might shut off any kind of creative thinking.

School library media specialists may wish to begin the sessions by providing clues to the listeners about the type of literature to be shared. A statement such as, "Today we are going to read a fairy tale. How do you think the story will begin?" may alert children to begin conceptualizing previously learned literary skills. Library media specialists may also decide to stop at some point and include another clue, saying, "Let's see if you can remember one of the three wishes," or ". . . one of the three objects that the hero must bring back." In setting the stage for these listening experiences they immediately provide students with some points of reference, which can lead to very rewarding follow-up discussions.

A little reminder. Since folktales are mostly based on oral traditions, they should be passed along to listeners by word of mouth rather than through the intermediary use of a filmstrip. A filmstrip simply cannot replace the human voice which creates a special aura of magic between the teller and listener. Children already who have been overly exposed to visual media need to experience this special interaction between storyteller and listeners, so that they too may at some time in the future carry forward this very old literary practice.

IDEA: How to share fables without "preaching." In sharing fables with children, school library media specialists may prefer to search for picture-book versions of fables that have been introduced in the basal reader. In studying fables, children are expected to observe that these stories can teach lessons and that they often present animals that have the ability to talk. Like fairy tales, fables need to be shared orally. Although a fable does teach a lesson, the lesson should not be overstressed but allowed to take hold of the listener on its own merit.

The sharing of the various illustrated versions of such fables as *The Hare and the Tortoise* will make for reading experiences and viewing experiences which children will long remember. Excellent editions of this fable include one illustrated by Brian Wildsmith and a contemporary modernized version called *Harry and Shellburt* by Dorothy O. Van Woerkom. Other illustrated versions of fables that are especially suitable for this learning level are Arnold Lobel's *Fables*, winner of the 1981 Caldecott award; Paul Galdone's humorous illustrated interpretation of *Three Aesop Fox Fables*, Richard Scarry's droll interpretation of *The Fables of LaFontaine*, Eric Carle's special bright version of *Twelve Tales from Aesop*, and Jack Kent's much smaller, cartoon-like interpretation of *More Fables of Aesop*.

IDEA: Building reading skills with informational books. Informational books have great appeal for first graders because at this age they still possess that special ingredient called curiosity. Reading skills of individual children will be greatly enhanced if children are allowed to look at and read informational books that suit their own needs. They will even apply themselves far more diligently during their reading lessons once they have discovered that learning to read means having the opportunity to read informational books which they have been able to select.

Fortunately for today's young readers, more and more informational books are being published with reading levels, comprehension levels, and interest levels suitable to the beginning reader's talents and interests. *Truck* and *Freight Train*, written and illustrated by Donald Crews, are superb samples of informational books which use only key words or short sentences, which beginning readers will not find too difficult to tackle. His unique, bold illustrative technique provides the beginning reader with the picture clues they need to interpret the informational concepts presented in the text.

Tana Hoban is another author/artist who has created informational books that are enticing to beginning readers. Her imaginative photographic illustrations and bold captions in *Push, Pull, Empty, Full: A Book of Opposites* and *Count and See* work like magnets to draw the eyes of the reader to each page. *Machines*, written and illustrated by the Rockwells, is also sure to please any beginning reader interested in learning how pulleys, gears, ball bearings, and sprockets function. Children fascinated by dinosaurs will find Peggy Parish's book, *Dinosaur Time*, just right for their beginning reading skills. The more skilled reader and young scientist will find Millicent E. Selsam's book, *Benny's Animals and How He Put Them in Order*, and Janet Chenery's *Wolfie* informative and challenging for further research projects.

Young readers who want to delve into books with detailed information about specific animals will find the books based on the Oxford Scientific Films most appropriate. Titles such as *Dragonflies* and *Common Frog* can be highly recommended for their beautifully detailed illustrations and precise text. Children who like to read and "do" things will find *The Berenstain Bears' Science Fair* by the Berenstains, as well as *Mickey's Magnet* by Branley and Vaughn to their particular liking.

The foregoing books are only a few choice examples of informational books that have a reading and interest level appropriate for this grade level. In searching for other books it is recommended that both the easy section and the pure and applied science section be searched to locate all available materials.

Ideas for Classroom or Library Media Center Use

The following ideas are suitable for use in either the library media center or the classroom. All are based on the use of library media center materials, but in some cases the possibilities for more frequent use and greater reinforcement afforded by the classroom will make them especially useful to the teacher there.

IDEA: Give the teacher a bagful of books. The nicest gift that a first grade teacher could receive from the school library media specialist at the beginning of the school year would be a paper bag filled with five to ten read-aloud picture books. A brown grocery bag tied with a perky ribbon will make this a perfect gift for teachers who need resources to help them create order out of turmoil during the first few weeks of the school year.

This gift can be tied in to the basal reader used in the first grade if the librarian takes an extra minute to select books from which the basal presents excerpts or books which have been suggested as enrichment reading. The selection of books could also be based on the overall theme of a particular basal. For instance, one basal, published by Macmillan, is called *Rainbow World*, so the library media specialist may wish to select the following books for the teacher's book bag:

> Freeman, Don. *A Rainbow of My Own*; il. by the author. New York: Viking, 1966.
> The beauty and magnificence of a rainbow are experienced by a little boy. A childhood classic not to be missed by any child.
> Ginsburg, Mirra. *Mushrooms in the Rain*; adapted from the Russian V. Suteyev; il. by Jose Aruego and Ariane Dewey. New York: Macmillan, 1974.
> Inclement weather helps a menagerie of animals realize the need for sharing.
> Lionni, Leo. *Frederick*; il. by the author. New York: Pantheon, 1967. Dreary winter weather is brightened by Frederick who gathers sun rays and colors.
> Scheer, Julian, *Rain Makes Applesauce*; il. by Marvin Bileck. New York: Holiday, 1964.
> To relieve the tension of the classroom every child needs this kind of "silly talk." A picture book with endless possibilities for looking and building dreams.

Another book bag might be filled with books to help children adjust to school and remain patient when "learning to read" does not happen the first day:

> Berenstain, Stan and Jan. *The Berenstain Bears Go to School*; il. by the authors. New York: Random, 1978.
> A delightful way to let children know that they are not the only ones apprehensive about going to school.
> Cohen, Miriam. *When Will I Read?* il. by Lillian Hoban. New York: Greenwillow, 1977.
> A helpful book for children who have become impatient because they did not learn to read the first day of school.
> Hoban, Lillian. *Arthur's Prize Reader*; il. by the author. New York: Harper, 1978.

Challenges of reading are humorously resolved between brother and sister chimps.

Ungerer, Tomi. *Crictor*; il. by the author. New York: Harper, 1958.
Crictor will add the right touch of humor and fantasy to make learning to read a little easier.

Giff, Patricia Reilly. *Next Year I'll Be Special*; il. by Marylin Hafner. New York: Dutton, 1980.
Every child needs to know that he or she is very special.

Teachers and children also will certainly welcome a book bag filled with books that will help them understand the special problems and situations which come up in every classroom. Some titles for these trying times are:

Cohen, Miriam. *First Grade Takes a Test*; il. by Lillian Hoban. New York: Greenwillow, 1980.
An excellent book to prepare children for taking tests. Actual examples of test questions have been included.

Mosel, Arlene. *Tikki Tikki Tembo*; il. by Blair Lent. Holt, 1968.
A wise story for children who feel left out.

Noble, Trinka Hakes. *The Day Jimmy's Boa Ate the Wash*; il. by Steven Kellogg. New York: Dial, 1980.
A child's and a parent's viewpoint of a school outing.

Van Woerkom, Dorothy. *The Queen Who Couldn't Bake Gingerbread*; il. by Paul Galdone. New York: Knopf, 1975.
Wisdom and humor mix to show the listener that everyone has certain limitations.

Williams, Barbara. *Albert's Toothache*; il. by Kay Chorao. New York: Dutton, 1974.
A very special story of a misplaced toothache.

IDEA: A new look at words through riddles, puzzles, and word books. Many basal readers include or suggest to teachers the use of puzzle or riddle books to help beginning readers recognize that words can be used in many different ways and for many different purposes. Although any time in the school year would be appropriate for using these books, the month of January, when the reading doldrums have sometimes set in, might be the most auspicious month to reach for special word books to create new reading excitement. To get the reading renewal program off to a humorous start, school library media specialists might wish to offer Jeanne and Margaret Wallace's *Really Ridiculous Rabbit Riddles*, which is filled with one-liners, to be shared by the teacher with the entire class; it can also be left in the reading corner for individualized reading. Steven Kroll's *Gobbleday Gook* is another funny book which will lead children to understand that a misplaced letter in a word can cause some rather unusual changes in its meaning.

For more advanced fun with words, including the study of homographs and homonyms, reach for *Fooling Around with Words* by Ruthven Tremain or Stoo Hample's *Yet Another Big Fat Funny Silly Book*, a book filled with not so silly ideas to help children increase their word knowledge through word lists, rhymes, riddles, and stories. For an especially joyous encounter with words, do not overlook Edith Baer's *Words Are Like Faces*. This miniature book is filled with many big ideas on the multitude of ways that words can be used.

Two riddle books which will surely motivate children to seek out additional reading materials are Jane Sarnoff's and Reynold Ruffins's *I Know! A Riddle Book* and *Giants! A Riddle Book*.

Teachers who want to add some internationalism to their word adventures will welcome Verna Aardema's *Ji-Nongo-Nongo Means Riddles*, an African riddle book, and *This Can Lick a Lollipop/Esto Gonza Chupando Un Caramelo: Body Riddles for Kids in English and Spanish* by Joel Rothman and Argentina Palacios.

Ideas for First Graders with Reading Problems

Since children reach reading readiness at various age levels, school library media specialists might suggest the following ideas to teachers with students who are already experiencing some reading problems at the first grade level.

IDEA: Taking alphabet walks with alphabet books. Select a group of special alphabet books and suggest that teachers use them with children who are experiencing difficulties learning their ABCs. *Alfred's Alphabet Walk*, a book written by Victoria Chess, is a very fine example of how an alphabet book can be used to show children that the alphabet plays a very important role in their daily lives. After Chess's book has been shared with the children, the teacher may be motivated to take them on school or neighborhood alphabet walks to find words that fit the specific letters designated for a particular day. Teachers might even make Alfred a class mascot who will cheer children on in their reading activities.

Other books that can be used for alphabet walks are *Adam's ABC*, by Adam Fife, an ABC story which tells about city life, and Idalia Rosario's *Idalia's ABC: An Urban Alphabet Book in English and Spanish*. For children who need to learn that letters of the alphabet come in all shapes, sizes, colors, and textures, Eric Carle's unique ABC book *All about Arthur* may be highly recommended. This book will be especially useful for students who need to use the tactile mode of learning the individual letters of the alphabet. Its format is texture oriented, which may inspire teachers to consider adapting Carle's ideas and concepts to create additional tactile experiences for their children. The various printed formats of the letters may be used to help young readers accept and perceive the various typefaces they encounter in their reading texts. In addition, the use of alliteration throughout the book is ideal for reinforcing concepts children often find difficult to learn.

For children who need to hear and see the alphabet reinforced through a story format, alphabet books such as Paula Sedgwick's *Circus ABC* and Wanda Gág's *The ABC Bunny* may be recommended. These books may also be used as stepping stones for the creation of teacher/child-made alphabet books.

IDEA: Word adventures with wordless picture books. Wordless picture books are an exciting medium for helping children develop and increase their language fluency. First grade children who have difficulty with sight words and basic decoding skills usually have a very meager language background and usually cannot associate abstract letter symbols with concrete objects. Learning to read for these children virtually comes to a standstill until they develop their language background and their ability to internalize abstract symbols. Although basal readers usually provide some remedial exercises for these readers, other creative ideas are needed to reach them. Wordless picture books are one viable medium through which children can expand their language abilities by first viewing and then trying to describe what they see.

Wordless picture books can be shared with children in the classroom as well as in the library media center. For small reading groups the wordless picture book can be held by the teacher, by the library media specialist, or it can be passed from child to child. If the teacher is working with a large reading group, an opaque projector should be used so that every child can have access to the image. Every child in the group should have the opportunity to look at and then talk about the pictures. Children should be encouraged to name the individual objects seen in the illustrations. They should, furthermore, be encouraged to speak in complete sentences so that their language skills will gradually develop towards expected norms.

In the classroom, after the book has been looked at in its entirety, the teacher should go back to the first page and begin to write out the words for the objects that children have named. After the names have been written, complete sentences should be written based on children's individual responses. It is very important that teachers emphasize that the words spoken by children can be put down on paper in letter symbols. Teachers need to make this point over and over again.

IDEA: How to use wordless picture books to develop basic vocabulary skills. Brinton Turkle's book *Deep in the Forest* could be used by school library media specialists to demonstrate to teachers how a wordless picture book can be tied in directly to the basic sight words which have been featured in the basal and the preprimer and primer level. Words such as *live, the, in, and, woods,* and *bears,* which have been included in several basals as basic vocabulary to be learned at this grade level, will certainly need to be used by children when trying to tell the story. In addition, this turnabout version of "Goldilocks and the Three Bears" will in itself be a worthwhile literary experience to which children should be introduced at this age.

Other wordless picture books that can be recommended for this type of language building activity are *The Snowman* by Raymond Briggs, *Pancakes for Breakfast* by Tomie DePaola, *Elephant Buttons* by Noriko Ueno, and *Bobo's Dream* by Martha Alexander.

How to Serve Early Readers

School library media specialists need to provide challenging reading materials for children who enter first grade with abilities beyond the expectations of the reading program. Children who are early readers in many instances become easily bored with the regular reading skills. In fact, some of the early readers sometimes vent their frustrations by simply refusing to participate in the regular lessons. What is more, some readers actually become regular discipline problems and finally reading "dropouts." To help prevent this, library media specialists should inform teachers of the many reading materials, appropriate and challenging for these students, that are in the school library media center. Teachers also should be informed that the library media center can supply books containing themes and topics describing the world from the viewpoint of the child of this age. This last point needs to be made, since it is all too tempting to give books to these children which are beyond their maturity level. We can, if not careful, cut short the time of childlike experiences that even early readers need in order to participate in the other group processes that are part of the first grade educational program.

Not all early readers read on the same level. In fact, the reading levels of early readers may spread from knowing a number of basic sight words to being able to read at the third or even fourth grade level. In very rare instances one even finds children who read beyond the fourth grade level.

Reading interests of early readers present another problem: many times they confine their reading interests to a very specialized area. In limiting their reading interests, early readers also confine their reading growth to that area. This can be very frustrating for the teachers and library media specialists who wish to open up the wider world of reading to these children. However, at this stage of reading development, it is far better to let beginning readers make their own reading choices so that they will not lose interest in developing their reading skills.

Suggested Books Appropriate for Early Readers

Books marketed as "I Can Read Books" or "Read-Alone Books" are very appropriate for children who enter first grade with a reading knowledge at about the level first graders usually acquire midway through the first grade. For instance, Harper and Row's very attractive series, under the imprint "I Can Read Books," includes a very wide variety of topics and styles, including animal fantasy, humor, and short plays. Two of Harper's more specialized series, which appear under the imprints of "An I Can Read History Book" and "A Nature I Can Read Book," should not be overlooked for their special appeal for children who are interested in exploring history or nature from a more serious point of view. Other publishers, too, market rather extensive lines of books for early readers. Dial is marketing a very attractively written and illustrated series called "Easy-to-Read" books. The numerous titles available in this series include both fantasy and realism. The "Read-Alone" series published by Greenwillow can also be recommended for its attractive format and wide variety of interesting topics. Macmillan publishes the "Ready-to-Read series, which covers a wide variety of fanciful topics, and the "Ready-to-Read Handbook" series, which deals with topics such as how to cook, how to do crafts, and the like.

First graders with approximately a second grade reading level will welcome the "A See and Read Book" series published by the Putnam Publishing Group. The series covers both fiction and informational topics. Coward, McCann and Geoghegan's "A Break-of-Day Book" series can also be recommended for the more advanced reader. Dutton's "Fat Cat" series, Pantheon's "I Am Reading" series, and Harcourt Brace Jovanovich's "A Let Me Read Book" series are also very appropriate for first graders with a second grade reading level. The Franklin Watts "Easy Read Fact Book" series can be recommended for children who have an advanced reading level and a very specialized interest in science.

First grade sleuths with a second grade reading capability will welcome the McGraw-Hill "Piet Potter Mystery" series as well as the Albert Whitman "First Read-Alone Mystery" series.

Children who are already reading on the third and fourth grade level may find books written by such well-known authors as Beverly Cleary, Carolyn Haywood, Alice Dalgliesh, Clyde Bulla, Natalie Savage Carlson, and Patricia Coombs to their liking. All have a very special talent of being able to develop stories with plots, themes, and characterizations which match the developmental level and interest and reading level of this age group.

Notes

1. Council on Interracial Books for Children, *Guidelines For Selecting Bias-Free Textbooks and Storybooks* (New York: The Association, n.d.).
2. Meredith Damien Gall. *Handbook for Evaluating and Selecting Curriculum Materials* (Boston: Allyn and Bacon, 1981).

Bibliography

Aardema, Verna. *Ji-Nongo-Nongo Means Riddles*; il. by Jerry Pinkney. New York: Four Winds, 1978.
Aesop. *Twelve Tales from Aesop*; told and il. by Eric Carle. New York: Philomel, 1980.
Alexander, Martha. *Bobo's Dream*; il. by the author. New York: Dial, 1978.
Baer, Edith. *Words Are Like Faces!* il. by Karen Gundersheimer. New York: Pantheon, 1980.
Berenstain, S. and J. *The Berenstain Bears' Science Fair*; il. by the authors. New York: Random, 1977.
Branley, Franklyn M. and Vaughan, Eleanor K. *Mickey's Magnet*; il. by Crocket Johnson. New York: Scholastic, 1956. (paper)
Briggs, Raymond. *The Snowman*. il. by the author. New York: Random, 1978.
Carle, Eric. *All about Arthur*; il. by the author. New York: Watts, 1974.

Chenery, Janet. *Wolfie*; il. by Marc Simon. (A Science I Can Read Book) New York: Harper, 1969.

Chess, Victoria. *Alfred's Alphabet Walk*; il. by the author. New York: Greenwillow, 1979.

Crews, Donald. *Freight Train*; il. by the author. New York: Greenwillow, 1978.

────. *Truck*; il. by the author. New York: Greenwillow, 1980.

DePaola, Tomie. *Pancakes for Breakfast*; il. by the author. New York: Harcourt, 1979.

Fife, Dale. *Adam's ABC*; il. by Don Robertson. New York: Coward, 1971.

Gág, Wanda. *The ABC Bunny*; il. by the author. New York: Coward, 1961.

Galdone, Paul. *Three Aesop Fox Fables*; il. by the author. New York: Seabury, 1971.

Hample, Stoo. *Yet Another Big Fat Funny Silly Book*; il. by the author. New York: Delacorte, 1980.

Hoban, Tana. *Count and See*; il. by the author. New York: Macmillan, 1972.

────. *Push-Pull, Empty Full: A Book of Opposites*; il. by the author. New York: Macmillan, 1972.

Kent, Jack. *More Fables of Aesop*; il. by the author. New York: Parents, 1974.

Kroll, Steven. *Gobbledy Gook*; il. by Kelly Oechsli. New York: Holiday, 1977.

La Fontaine, Jean de. *The Hare and the Tortoise*; il. by Brian Wildsmith. New York: Watts, 1967.

Lobel, Arnold. *Fables*; il. by the author. New York: Harper, 1980.

Oxford Scientific Films. *Common Frog*; il. by George Bernard. New York: Putnam, 1979.

────. *Dragonflies*; il. by George Bernard. New York: Putnam, 1980.

Parish, Peggy. *Dinosaur Time*; il. by Arnold Lobel. (An Early I Can Read Book) New York: Harper, 1974.

Rockwell, Anne and Harlow. *Machines*; il. by the authors. New York: Macmillan, 1972.

Rosario, Idalia. *Idalia's Project ABC: An Urban Alphabet Book in English and Spanish*; il. by the author. New York: Holt, 1981.

Rothman, Joel and Palacios. *This Can Lick A Lollipop/Esto Goza Chupando Un Caramelo*; il. by Patricia Ruben. New York: Doubleday, 1979.

Sarnoff, Jane and Ruffins, Reynold. *Giants! A Riddle Book*; il. by the authors. New York: Scribner, 1977.

Scarry, Richard. *The Fables of La Fontaine*; adap. and il. by Richard Scarry. New York: Doubleday, 1963.

Sedgwick, Paulita. *Circus ABC*; il. by the author. New York: Holt, 1978.

Selsam, Millicent E. *Benny's Animals and How He Put Them In Order*; il. by Arnold Lobel. (A Science I Can Read Book) New York: Harper, 1966.

Tremain, Ruthven. *Fooling Around with Words*; il. by the author. New York: Greenwillow, 1976.

Turkle, Brinton. *Deep in the Forest*; il. by the author. New York: Dutton, 1976.

Ueno, Noriko. *Elephant Buttons*; il. by the author. New York: Harper, 1973.

Van Woerkom, Dorothy O. *Harry and Shellburt*; il. by Erick Ingraham. New York: Macmillan, 1977.

Wallace, Jeanne and Margaret. *Really Ridiculous Rabbit Riddles*; il. by Dave Ross. New York: Walker, 1979.

5

Reading at the Second Grade Level (The Reader Begins to Fly)

Diversities of Abilities, Interests, and Attitudes

In the second grade young readers begin to "fly" with the reading "wings" they developed in the first grade. Of course, not every child is as ready as every other to read at the same speed or cover the same distance. Teaching them to read on their own is, in fact, immensely difficult, since the reading abilities of second graders already vary widely. A teacher may have to deal with children who read at the third, fourth, and even fifth grade level, as well as some whose reading abilities are barely adequate for the second grade.

Some of the diversity of reading abilities can be attributed to such factors as physical and mental maturity. Not all children enter the second grade at precisely the same age, and an age difference of a few months at this stage of the learner's development can sometimes be critical to the learner's ability to perform or conceptualize certain reading tasks. However, other factors such as attitude, home environment, learning environment, and cultural background can also influence classroom performance.

A negative attitude toward reading may develop in children who come from home environments in which reading is neither nurtured nor reinforced by a positive regard for the learner or the teacher. Yet the same negative attitude may also occur in homes where reading is highly valued. Sometimes that high regard is not communicated to children by adults who unthinkingly take it for granted that children recognize the importance of reading. Sibling rivalry, brought about by parents who unwittingly compare children's abilities without taking into consideration their individual interests and their physical and intellectual differences, may also be a contributing factor.

The demeanor of the classroom teacher also influences reading interests and attitudes. Teachers with positive, enthusiastic attitudes usually create classroom climates that encourage even reluctant readers to participate and to work up to their reading potentials.

These teachers usually surround their students with attractive classroom libraries. They encourage frequent use of the school library media center. They also make it a daily practice to read to their students, and they talk about books with such fervor that even the most reluctant readers cannot help but give reading a chance.

What is happening in the school outside the classroom can also shape reading behavior. Schools in which the principal is totally involved in the reading program and shares his or her own enthusiasm about books and reading with children usually record more successful reading programs than schools where there is little cooperation among principal, teachers, and students. Likewise, in schools in which principals and reading supervisors actively support the school library media center, reading attitudes and abilities have better chances to flourish than in schools where library media centers are treated more like appendages.

Managing the Different Reading Abilities

Managing the various reading abilities presents a tremendous challenge for classroom teachers who have to fit the standard second grade basal reader to the multitude of reading abilities found in the classroom. To find an equitable solution to this dilemma, many teachers group their children into so-called "ability" groups. What this means is that the teacher has three reading groups, high, medium, and low. Although such names as "red bird," "blue bird," and "black bird" for the groups have finally fallen by the wayside and now have been disguised with more contemporary terms, usually kinds of "achievers," children still are able to recognize their level of competence.

Assessing reading abilities. The grouping of children is usually based on scores on a standardized test, such as the S.R.A. Achievement Test, the Stanford Achievement Test, or the Metropolitan Achievement Test, administered by the school. These tests are norm referenced; that is, they provide information that compares the reading abilities of students. They are also survey tests: they survey a variety of reading skills, such as vocabulary knowledge and comprehension. There are, however, other standardized tests that are more diagnostic and that reveal more precisely reading weaknesses. Examples of these standard diagnostic tests are the Gates-McKillop Reading Diagnostic Test, the McCullough Word Analysis Test, and the Doren Diagnostic Reading Test of Word Recognition Skills.

Many schools supplement their standardized testing with teacher-made tests. The advantage of a teacher-made test is that it permits measurement of individual children's reading abilities when the need arises.

One of the most popular teacher-made tests is called the IRI, or Informal Reading Inventory. The IRI is developed by teachers with the reading materials presently being used in the school. The test itself consists of two parts: the oral part which measures the oral reading ability of students and the silent part which measures the comprehension level of students.

The results of the IRI test indicate at what level the students in a teacher's classroom are reading. For instance, if a student is able to read orally a designated 100-word excerpt with fewer than three mistakes and is able to answer the comprehension questions on the silent portion of the test with equal success, the teacher knows that the student is reading at the independent level. If, however, the student makes five mistakes on the oral portion and three mistakes on the silent comprehension portion, the student is reading at the instructional level. In cases where students make considerably more than five mistakes on either the oral or silent portion of the test, they are reading at the frustration level. The oral portion is also a diagnostic tool for teachers, because students, while reading aloud, reveal how well they can apply the different word attack skills.

Not all students who perform poorly on the oral portion of the test perform poorly on the silent portion. The school library media specialist can double-check the reading abilities of these students by asking them to read orally from a book generally believed to be too advanced for the readers. Students who make numerous mistakes reading aloud may do so because they are under considerable pressure, not because they lack the necessary reading skills.

Of course, the results of the IRI are subject to error. Many teachers, therefore, retest students who have shown poor results in order to validate their findings.

Other arrangements for grouping students. The fear that ability grouping would hinder children from working towards performance beyond their designated group level has led some teachers to try a heterogeneous approach to grouping, in the hope that the outstanding readers would challenge the slower readers. Although this scheme has some merit, it has also raised some doubts about detrimental effects that such groupings might have on the advanced readers.

Some school districts have tried regrouping entire grade levels into ability groups. This means that children from all second grade classes would leave their classrooms at an appointed time and go to a designated teacher who would teach a certain ability group. Although it might be desirable to have children come under the tutelage of different teachers, second graders as a whole do not always have the maturity to deal with the class changes, teacher changes, and time changes.

All these arrangements raise the question, "What happens to children who are gifted readers?" Despite the renewed awareness of the plight of gifted readers, not enough is being done at present to help them. Most school districts place these special readers in what are called "top" reading groups. However, these groups might contain children who read one year above their reading levels along with those who read two to three years above level. The materials used with these children range from basals on advanced levels to self-pacing materials, such as those created by Science Research Associates and Reader's Digest. Some schools also allow their gifted students special computer access to practice word attack and comprehension skills. However, most schools still prefer to use basal readers with their gifted students because of the need to keep even those children within the structure of the regular reading program.

Teaching Reading Skills in the Second Grade

Teaching methods for second grade reading are very similar to those for the first grade. At the beginning of the school year, considerable time is usually devoted to reviewing skills learned in the first grade but forgotten during the long summer vacation. If the basal reader approach is used, the teacher continues to teach word attack skills, comprehension skills, literary skills, language skills, and study skills. The difficulty of the skills, as might be expected, increases with each grade level. For instance, while first graders learned primarily how to decode one-syllable words, second graders learn how to decode multisyllabic words.

In the area of comprehension, second graders are also gradually introduced to more complex skills. More emphasis is placed on the application of critical and creative thinking skills. These skills are usually taught through discussion based on questions suggested by the teacher handbook for the basal series. The questions are usually shared with children before they read a selection silently so that they will have a purpose for reading the story. The questions are later discussed by the teacher and students during the oral portion of the reading lesson. Comprehension skills are usually reinforced and tested by asking students to answer true or false or multiple choice questions in the basal workbooks.

Completing workbook pages is adequate for reinforcing literal comprehension; however, it falls far short in teaching critical or creative comprehension. The shortcoming of how comprehension is taught in many classrooms has already evidenced itself in recent national reading test scores. It seems to be the general consensus that when reading scores declined, more emphasis was placed on word attack skills, while comprehension skills were shortchanged.

Other factors also contribute to the decline of comprehension skills. Many basal texts are not providing teachers with the type of literature or instructions which would lead both teachers and students toward developing higher comprehension skills. Some teachers also neglect the teaching of these skills because their educational training lacked background in how to initiate teaching of comprehension skills through the use of skillful questioning techniques. Comprehension skills are usually also neglected in school districts that operate under very tight time schedules, especially in schools that operate under a system called "pacing." The pacing system requires that a certain number of reading assignments be covered during a specified time period. Although pacing would seem to be a very efficient method of guiding children through their reading lessons, it fails to take into consideration the various learning capacities of children, which rarely coincide with deadlines.

Literary skills are usually taught in conjunction with comprehension skills. Most basal readers suggest that second graders learn how to identify literary selections as either fiction or nonfiction. It is also generally suggested that second graders learn to distinguish the literary techniques of first and third person narration. Even the concept of looking for "main" ideas has been introduced in some second grade basal readers.

As was mentioned previously, study skills and library media center skills are not necessarily distinguished by the basal publishers. Under study skills, second graders are taught how to alphabetize up to the second letter within a word, so that they may begin to learn how to use the dictionary. In teaching dictionary skills considerable emphasis is placed on the use and function of guide words. Second graders are also introduced to the use of the glossary and are expected to be able to differentiate between the functions of dictionaries and glossaries by the end of the second grade. Map reading skills are also introduced at this level. Children are taught how to use scales on a map and cardinal directions when using a globe.

Although one might classify all the skills just mentioned as library media center reference skills, most basal companies do not make specific suggestions that teachers use school library media center resources to teach these skills. Study skills, as such, are usually introduced by the teacher through a teaching demonstration and written directions on the chalkboard. The skills are then practiced by students through completion of workbook exercises or exercises on ditto sheets. This approach, however, is limited in how it can truly teach and reinforce skills, since it does not involve practical applications. The use of the library media center to teach and strengthen these skills would immeasurably enrich the learning experiences of second graders.

Students will become better readers if and when they are encouraged to use the rich treasures of the school library media center to practice their individual "flying"styles of studying and reading.

6

Role of the School Library Media Specialist in the Second Grade Reading Program

The role of the school library media specialist in the second grade reading program can be summarized in the statement, "Keep them reading at all costs so that they will learn to read with confidence." Providing books and other reading matter is simple enough, but library media specialists need to do far more to keep second graders reading. They must excite children to open up the books they check out of the library. They also need to inspire children to take the prospect of independent reading seriously and to form reading habits that will open doors to treasures for a lifetime. The charge, "to keep them reading," also requires that school library media specialists come forth with reading activities which will fit the needs of children who lack confidence or skill as well as those who are already independent readers. Learning to read requires that reader and library media specialists meet and share the delights of reading in an encouraging environment.

How to Discover Reading Interests of Second Graders

To help second graders become enthusiastic and proficient readers, library media specialists must first of all ask that all-important question, "What do second graders really like to read?" Research on the reading interests of children provides some answers. Particularly good summaries of this type of research are found in Helen Huus's book, *Evaluating Books for Children and Young People*[1] and Purves and Beach's book, *Literature and the Reader*.[2] Journal literature on current reading interest research and sample reading interest surveys may be located through *Education Index* or ERIC.

Recent Reading Interest Research Findings

Reading interests of children are influenced by a number of factors. Those most frequently mentioned are age, sex, intelligence of the reader, and the reading environment (including availability of materials and format of the book). As age increases, children's experiences are enlarged, and so their reading interests expand in scope. For this reason, children in the second grade have relatively limited reading interests. Sex of the reader does not influence reading interests until about age nine, according to most studies. In second grade, therefore, boys and girls show little difference in reading interests.

Intelligence of the reader influences reading interests in terms of the variety and depth of topics selected. It might also influence the number of books read. Bright children tend to develop more divergent reading interests earlier than children of lesser intelligence.

Reading environment, availability of materials, and book format also influence reading interests. For example, reading interests are nurtured in home, classroom, school library media center, and public library environments that give children ample access to a wide variety of reading materials.

The format of the book, particularly its illustrations, text, shape, and size, also makes it attractive or unattractive to the young reader. Young children prefer, for instance, illustrations with clear and precise outlines and distinct colors. Contrary to some popular belief, it is not always the larger book that is of interest to younger children. Smaller, palm-sized books which can be held snugly by tiny hands are also very appealing to children of this age group.

As far as the text is concerned, second graders prefer stories which have exciting beginnings and middles and satisfactory conclusions. Flashbacks are not well liked at this age level; neither are books that convey a particular mood very popular with children at this grade level. Second graders prefer humorous and nonsensical stories with much action and with characters who carry the story line through breathtaking adventures. They also prefer endings that leave them with a new zest for reading as well as a new viewpoint.

Some shortcomings of reading interest research. School library media specialists can gain an overall perspective on children's reading interests from a perusal of this research. However, as most studies point out, each study has certain limitations which affect its application to any particular audience. The limitations might be in the area of the audience studied, geographic location of the study, or even media events during the time of the study. Reading interests in a particular community may be influenced by viewpoints fostered there; whether they are conservative or liberal, the viewpoints may render the interest study invalid for a larger or different audience.

Reading interest studies easily become dated if the interests measured are affected by events in the popular media either before or during the study. For example, books on sharks were undoubtedly more popular while the movie *Jaws* was a box office hit.

Another possible limitation is the format of the published study. If only an abstract is available, the report of important variables, such as specific geographical location and makeup of the audience, may be so abbreviated that the reader cannot determine if the results might be applicable. Considering some of the limitations of research studies that have been done on a regional or even national level, library media specialists should probably use the studies only as guidelines and proceed to create their own surveys of the reading interests of their patrons. A combined evaluation of the published and the original studies may then make the data of both far more useful.

How to Prepare Simple Reading Interest Surveys

Reading interest surveys (also called reading interest inventories) should be short, should use vocabulary familiar to second graders, and should be prepared so that second graders can complete them without too much teacher assistance. (Appendixes B and C provide sample surveys for elementary school children.) The questions used for the study should be worded in such a manner that they do not intimidate or pressure children into answers that do not represent their real likes or dislikes.

One reading teacher who prepared a reading-interest survey for her second-graders found that a questionnaire which lists twelve types of children's stories satisfactory. The questions were phrased in the following manner: "I like to read about pets" (best — sometimes — least). "I like to read about wild animals" (best — sometimes — least), etc.[3] Library media specialists who find such terms as "pets" still too broad to learn the real likes and dislikes of children might refine the terminology more, asking specific questions such as, "Do you like to read about dogs?" (yes — no), "Do you like to read about dinosaurs?" (yes — no), and "Do you like to read about ghosts?" (yes — no).

If teachers and school library media specialists want to find out more about the children's reading environment outside the school, a question such as, "Does anyone read to you at home?" (yes — no) might provide some clues. During the last few years more and more research has pointed out that children who have been exposed to few read-aloud experiences at home usually show less enthusiasm for reading than their peers who have been nurtured with many read-aloud experiences. Library media specialists who need to find out even more about the home reading environment may include additional questions, such as, "Do you get a newspaper at home?" (yes — no), "Have you ever received a book as a gift?" (yes — no), "Have you ever bought a book on your own?" (yes — no), and "Do you go to the public library to get books?" (yes — no).

Since television viewing habits can also influence the reading interests of children, reading interest surveys should also make an attempt to ask questions that will measure this factor. Questions such as, "Would you rather watch television?" (yes — no), "What is your favorite TV program?" (name of program), and "How many hours of TV are you allowed to watch each evening" (1 — 2 — 3) will not only tell much about the habits of children out of school, but also will indicate to teachers and school library media specialists what media influence they must interact with and, often, counter.

After the reading interest inventories have been administered, and teacher and library media specialist have tallied their responses, plans can be made to develop a reading program which focuses not only on the areas of particular interest to children but also on areas of interest to teachers, which they might use for remedial purposes.

Ideas for Implementing the Second Grade Reading Program

The following pages present various ideas which can be used to encourage second graders to become successful readers. The ideas range from read-aloud experiences to reading tutors programs to the use of puppets.

IDEA: Turning read-aloud bibliographies into read-alone bibliographies. Bibliographies suggesting read-aloud books for second grade teachers could provide a sound beginning. Since reading interest surveys indicate that second graders seem enthusiastic about stories that center around nonsense, humor, and make-believe, bibliographies should focus on these areas.

Because most schools usually have more than one section of second graders, two or three bibliographies should be prepared so that ample materials will be available for each group. Books recommended on these bibliographies should be set aside so that teachers may be able to pick them up as a set and make them readily available in their classrooms for a period of time.

Teachers should also be encouraged to let children use the read-aloud books as supplementary readers so that they will have access to reading matter other than their basals. The books listed should, therefore, be at approximately the second grade reading level.

The basal reader is another source of titles for the bibliography of read aloud books. As was mentioned earlier, the teachers' edition of t1e basal usually lists a bibliography marked "books for children to read by themselves." Some publishers also have printed separate bibliographies of the suggested books, usually available free of charge from the publishers.

IDEA: Developing reading units with teachers. School library media specialists and teachers may sit down and develop specific reading units on topics most appealing to children. The reading interest inventory previously described is particularly helpful here, especially if it was focused on relatively specific topics, such as, "Do you like to read books about dinosaurs?" and "Do you like to read about ghosts?"

Early planning of these special interest units is necessary. The school library media center's collection in the special interest areas may have to be strengthened to complement whatever approaches the reading unit might take. Therefore, units need to be planned at least one semester, perhaps even a year, before implementation so that materials can be acquired. Duplicate copies may also be ordered so that enough materials will be on the shelves to serve larger groups of children.

If, for example, a unit on dinosaurs is considered, library media specialists and teachers might plan a unit which, although primarily print oriented, also uses some audiovisual materials. These supplemental materials will highlight information which might otherwise not be comprehensible to the reader. Library media specialists may also be able to suggest realia, which could be secured from a local or regional museum. Checking the library media center's community resource file may even reveal an authority on dinosaurs who could be invited to introduce the unit. The unit itself might be divided into the following categories:

Factual Information About Dinosaurs
  Types of dinosaurs
    bipeds
    quadrupeds
    carnivorous
    herbivorous
    hot-blooded
    cold-blooded
  Dinosaur fossils
    Size and shape of fossils
      fossils in nature
      fossils in the museum
    Dinosaur-related reptiles
  Fantasy (what if??)
    Where would dinosaurs live today?
    What if I had a dinosaur as a pet?
    What would it cost to feed a dinosaur today?

After children have explored the various areas of dinosaur fact and lore, the unit might culminate in the following activities which can be completed by the children either individually or as a group project.

Children draw a dinosaur-size mural (to be hung on several walls in the school) based on books that have been read
Children write a news report on a newly discovered dinosaur
Children write a three- to four-line dinosaur story
Children create recipes for feeding a dinosaur
Children make dinosaur footprints which lead to the school library media center and list a dinosaur book title on each footprint
Children are taken on a field trip to a museum
Children construct a dinosaur.

Another unit that may appeal to second graders could be based on the topic of monsters, ghosts, and dragons. Such a unit would have greater appeal, of course, during the autumn months and could be completed in time for Halloween. The unit might first emphasize the humorous aspects of monsters, ghosts, and dragons, and then proceed to the more "haunted" theme found in folktales.

To add a touch of real spookiness to the unit, teachers and library media specialists could construct a monster's den or haunted house in the school library media center or classroom.

After Halloween, the monster den can be converted to a reading area to give children some privacy and a special atmosphere for reading their books.

The unit may be completed by asking children to carry out the following written activities:

Develop recipes for feeding the monster
Write a booklet on how to care for the monster
Develop a reading list for the monster
Write a monster story or book.

IDEA: Provide a reading corner with a puppet to read to. Many teachers have discovered that some second graders who are not performing well in groups nevertheless put forth considerably more effort when they read to a large puppet in a reading corner. In a situation like this, young readers soon begin to gain confidence, because they are challenged to provide a service to someone else. Children and puppets seem to have a very special way of communicating with each other. Teachers who have tried this report that it has boosted the ego of their reluctant readers and has also made the readers more aware of their reading problems and eager to remedy them through additional effort. The reading corner can be created either in the classroom or in a quiet corner of the school library media center.

There are several ways of selecting the reading matter to be used in the reading corner. The young readers may use books they select on their own, or they may choose from books placed in the reading corner by the teacher or library media specialist. (For this purpose such books as the "I Can Read" and "Read Alone" titles are good choices.) The child could also be asked to read a book that the teacher or library media specialist has placed in the hands of the puppet—in this way the puppet is encouraging the reader to participate by reading a book the puppet wants to hear.

IDEA: Have second graders read to kindergarten children. Some teachers and school library media specialists have also discovered that children with low self-esteem and severe reading problems improve their reading skills considerably when they read to a group of kindergarten children.

The children who are going to read first of all observe a read-aloud experience presented either by the kindergarten teacher or the library media specialist. Next, either teacher or library media specialist helps each child select a book to read to the kindergarten group. The second graders then practice for the read-aloud experience. Once comfortable with the reading material, each child can either tape the read-aloud experience or read the story to the teacher or library media specialist. This step is important, since it will provide the opportunity to give the reader additional hints on how to improve the experience. Perhaps a child may need to be told how to hold the book during the reading, or how to control the rate of reading so that younger children are able to follow the story line, or how to prepare for the opening of the read-aloud experience and how to close it.

If the first reading does not go as well as expected, it is important to reassure the reader and invite him or her for a return reading experience. It is particularly important that the child not lose faith or interest in reading at this time. The real value of this read-aloud experience should be measured both in the success that the reader may experience and also in how the kindergarten children respond to the reading of a slightly older child.

IDEA: Use volunteer reading tutors to help second grade readers. A volunteer reading tutor program, administered through the school library media center, can be an invaluable service to second graders. This program has worked especially well for children who cannot keep up with the pace set for them in the classroom. It has also been the right medicine for children who need an extra warm smile, a special hug, and many extra words of encouragement to keep them performing on level. In addition, the program may work miracles for children who are relatively unattended in their homes and need someone to encourage their reading. The use of both male and female tutors has certain advantages, because it can satisfy the needs of children searching for a father or mother figure.

Reading tutors for gifted readers. The use of reading tutors need not be limited to helping problem readers. The bright minds of gifted readers sometimes get lost in classrooms which are overwhelmed with students who are barely keeping up with the daily reading requirements. Gifted readers can be helped considerably if they are assigned to reading tutors who have the time and patience to listen to the special reading needs the gifted may have. One of these needs is usually a desire to discuss and elaborate in great detail on the material they have read. In many classrooms, little time is left for such elaborate discussions, and because of this situation gifted students not only feel neglected, sometimes they themselves become problem readers. Tutors can take the time to listen to the gifted readers and even discuss with them some of the creative ideas that have come about through their reading. Tutors can also help gifted readers by guiding them toward books that will present additional new ideas and viewpoints. The goal of the reading tutor should be to help prevent gifted readers from becoming reluctant readers.

Reading tutors for dyslexic children. Dyslexic children are usually assigned to special reading classes. They also may be helped by tutors who have the time to read stories from basal readers to them. Because dyslexic children have perception and reversal problems, many have learned to compensate for this neurological disorder by becoming good listeners and developing good memories. Children, therefore, who have someone who reads the material to them orally can, in many cases, rejoin the regular classroom reading groups for at least some of the comprehension and discussion lessons. Becoming part of the regular group is of great importance to these children, who are not mentally disabled but only handicapped in one particular area.

How to select reading tutors. Reading tutors need to be carefully selected, since not everyone has the patience to work with younger children. For example, not even former teachers are necessarily effective reading tutors. Who, then, are the best reading tutors? They are people who enter the school library media center with bright smiles. They are people who reach out with loving arms, take a discouraged child by the hand, and find a corner in which to sit and read to him or her. They are people who do not give up on children who keep stumbling over the same simple words. They are people who, when overhearing teachers remarking, "This child is from my lowest group," firmly reply, "But not for long." Library media specialists usually are able to discover whether a volunteer will be a good tutor by observing her or him reading to children. Volunteers who are animated readers, full of enthusiasm and patience when children have all too many questions, usually turn out to be good tutors.

Reading tutors, on the other hand, should not be expected to be experts in the teaching of reading. They should use their own alternate methods to cure the reading ailments with which second graders are afflicted.

IDEA: Teaching dictionary skills. Dictionary skills can be reinforced in the school library media center. The library media specialist may set up a learning center, in which different stations are used for practicing different dictionary skills.

Station 1:   Learning to alphabetize letter by letter.

How: Student places alphabet cards in correct order.

Self-checking: Provide students with a sheet listing the alphabet. Students who make more than five mistakes will be asked to repeat the assignment.

Station 2:   Learning to alphabetize words up to the second letter.

How: Student places 15 or 20 word cards in alphabetical order.

Self-checking: Provide student with a copy of the master answer sheet. Students who make more than five mistakes will be asked to repeat the exercise.

Station 3:   Learning about the function of guide words in a dictionary.

How: Student listens to a tape that explains guide words while using a dictionary to follow along with the explanation.

Station 4:   Learning to use guide words in a dictionary.

How: Student is given ten word cards and asked to write down on a separate sheet of paper the guide words found in the dictionary on the page that contains each word. (For example, word card: BADGE; guide words: bacon—bagpipe.)

Station 5:   Can you beat the clock?

How: Students are timed when looking up words in a dictionary. This approach reinforces the usefulness of guide words in the dictionary.

IDEA: Teaching map skills in the library media center. Library media specialists can reinforce map skills by using a map of the school library media center to introduce children to the arrangement of the media center. To build on the map skills that children have learned in the regular classroom lesson, librarians may follow these teaching steps:

1. Place large piece of white paper on an easel.
2. Discuss with children how maps are created.
3. With the help of the children, begin drawing a map of the school library media center. Location of the card catalog, circulation desk, reference shelf, etc., may be good starting points.

4. Place symbols for tables and chairs on the map. Ask children to devise symbols to identify these items for the library media center user.
5. Give a small scale map of the media center to each child.
6. Ask each child to examine the map and tell whether any changes are needed and whether the symbols are clear enough for the user to find what he or she needs.

During the following weeks library media specialists may wish to introduce the city map to children and help them locate the streets they live on. They may also wish to help children find specific places of interest, such as the zoo, museum, stadium, and the like. The state map may be introduced at the culmination of the unit.

IDEA: Help children differentiate between fiction and nonfiction books. Library media specialists can reinforce the discrimination of fiction from nonfiction through some of the following school library media center activities: When planning read-aloud experiences for children, select both fiction and nonfiction books. When reading to children, open the session by briefly reviewing why a book is called fiction or nonfiction. Share with children that a fiction book is a story created by an author using characters, settings (places) that are not real but are invented by the author. To explain the term nonfiction, library media specialists may say that the author describes people, places, or objects that are real. Upon completion of the read-aloud experience solicit answers from students that might explain why the story that was just read is either fiction or nonfiction.

IDEA: Getting the home involved in the reading process. The following ideas may be implemented if reading inventories reveal that children have little access to books and other reading matter at home.

1. Send home a letter to parents encouraging parents to read to their children, so that reading levels may be raised. Include a read-aloud bibliography in the letter. Also alert parents that books may be available to them through the school library media center, the public library, or in book stores. A sample letter is provided in Appendix A.
2. Ask the PTA/PTO to sponsor a program that alerts parents to the benefits of reading aloud to children on a daily basis.

In planning the program the school library media specialist may wish to invite a reading teacher to open the program by presenting a brief overview of positive research results that points out the benefits of a home read-aloud program. The library media specialist may follow this presentation with a few hints for parents on how to read aloud. An actual read-aloud demonstration, using a humorous book, should also be included to help parents realize that reading aloud is not difficult, but can be a truly rewarding family experience. If at all possible, the school library media specialist may even ask some parents to share with other parents how reading aloud to their children has enriched the reading skills of their youngsters. The program may be closed by presenting parents with a read-aloud bibliography and information about where the books may be secured.

3. Sponsor a book fair where parents may purchase books to share with their children or to give as gifts to encourage children to develop their own home library. The book fair may be planned any time during the year. However, a fair scheduled prior to Christmas may encourage parents to purchase books as Christmas gifts. The fair may be planned through the cooperation of a local book distributor, a local bookstore, or a company specializing in sponsoring book fairs.

4. Sponsor a "read-in" at a local shopping mall to show parents the importance of reading. The read-in may be carried out in a special community room set aside by the mall or in the community room some larger department stores provide. If neither facility is available, a regular area within the mall may have to be used. The read-in experience should include storytellers as well as story readers. The program should include stories for all age levels, even adults. Both children and parents should be encouraged to listen and participate in the storytelling and reading experience. Special reading exhibits should also be placed throughout the mall. The exhibitors may include the public library, reading specialists from the local school district, the International Reading Association and other public organizations interested in the promotion of reading and literacy. A special area may also be set aside for a paperback book exchange for both children and adults.

5. Ask local newspapers to run a special feature on why parents need to read to their children. For smaller towns the

editor responsible for local news may have to be contacted. In larger cities the editor responsible for educational news may be contacted. Local radio station talk shows may also be approached for special interviews on why it is important that parents read to children.

6. Cooperate with your public library to develop a summer reading program. To initiate the program establish contact with your public library children's librarian and discuss the possibilities of cooperation. Invite the children's librarian to come to your school and explain to the children what special reading programs are available to them during the summer months. The public librarian may even wish to issue library card applications for children who do not have a card.

Notes

1. Helen Huus, *Evaluating Books for Children and Young People* (Newark, Del.: International Reading Assn., 1968). Perspectives in Reading no. 10.

2. Alan C. Purves and Richard Beach, *Literature and the Reader: Research in Response to Literature Reading Interests and the Teaching of Reading* (Urbana, Ill.: National Council of Teachers of English, 1972).

3. Angeline Stalma, "Reading interests of second-graders, revealed!" *Early Years* 11:75 (May 1981).

7

Reading at Third through Fifth Grade Levels (The Reader Flies Alone)

Beginning with the third grade, and continuing in the fourth and fifth grades, students learn to "fly" alone, to read independently and develop individual tastes. During these years, students discover the unlimited reading adventures available to them through the printed word. The independent "flight" patterns students set for themselves during these years are, of course, still regulated by such factors as their attitude toward the printed word, their mental ability, chronological age, sex, physical well-being, and the reading environments at home and school.

The Appearance of Special Reading Interests

It is in the third grade that children begin to be more selective and verbal in their reading likes and dislikes. Boys, for example, seem to take an enormous interest in war books and books of an informational nature. Girls, while not particularly interested in war books, will read informational books. However, their interests at this grade level also begin to lean very much towards books which delve into the problems of growing up female. Girls also prefer books which describe friendships and have slight touches of romance. Even though there seem to be differences in what boys and girls like to read, there are also still reading interests which they share. Of particular interest to both boys and girls are joke books, riddle books, books which contain slapstick humor, animal stories, stories of modern fantasy, and science fiction. Reading research has also discovered that it is at this grade level that both boys and girls become increasingly more aware of the quality of literature they are reading. Children who were interviewed were quite capable of expressing a desire to read books which have a good plot and character development.

Reading interests during these grade levels are also very much dictated by popular events, popular movies, and the likes and dislikes of a popular hero. Special "in" groups within a classroom or within the school may also be very influential as to what books are considered popular reading.

The influence that teachers and library media specialists have on reading interests depends largely on the relationship they may have with the children. Those who read to the children and talk enthusiastically about books can do much to stimulate children to develop their reading habits and their reading interests. The value of carefully planned storytelling programs should not be overlooked. Although the influence of a storyteller has not been scientifically documented, it is well known that storytellers have the magic touch to open up the wider world of reading.

Principals who have made an all-out effort to promote reading in their schools by supporting the school library media center, encouraging special reading programs, and sharing the delights of reading with their students, have also directly influenced the attitudes that children may have towards reading.

The influence that the home has on shaping children's reading interests must also not be overlooked. Parents who have supported and encouraged their children's reading habits by reading to them, buying books for them, and taking them to the library have done their part to shape their children's reading interests.

Researching the reading interests of children is not easy. Many studies have concluded that it is very difficult to come up with findings which are not somewhat influenced by variables such as the number of children interviewed, cultural makeup of the children, the type of instrument used, and the method in which the survey was administered. However, despite the difficulty of collecting the research data, certain major trends have emerged from numerous research studies which have been carried out over the years. For example, prior to 1960, many of the studies concluded that differences in reading interests were dictated by an innate desire of boys to read masculine books and an innate desire of girls to read feminine books. Current research, however, seems to propose that reading interests may also be brought about by cultural training. This interesting finding was presented by Schofer in an investigation which compared interests of British children with American children. The study concluded that "there is less difference in children's reading preferences between sex, age, and nationality than we, as educators, have been led to believe by previous studies."[1]

Whether the new findings reflect the fact that more and more schools are emphasizing a nonsexually differentiated curriculum or that they reflect new investigative techniques is still uncertain. In any case, school library media specialists and teachers need to keep abreast of research so that they may develop reading programs which will guide children toward becoming independent lifelong readers.

Teaching Reading at Third through Fifth Grades

The teaching of reading in grades three through five follows essentially the same teaching format established in earlier grades. Preparation for reading, silent reading, oral reading, decoding skills, and comprehension skills are practiced on a daily basis. However, the relative intensity with which the particular skills are practiced changes. For instance, oral reading, which dominated much of the reading lesson in first and second grades, is practiced far less in the fourth and fifth grades. Now the development of comprehension skills and silent reading receive more and more emphasis. Far more attention is also placed on the development of study/library media center skills and literary skills in these grades. Silent reading and comprehension skills are usually practiced by the students by completing workbook pages. Study/library media center skills and literary skills are taught by the teacher through teacher/student discussions and are practiced and reinforced through the completion of workbook pages. Some basal readers also suggest more practice may be achieved by the reading of additional books which may be secured from the school library media center. These books are usually recommended under special teaching suggestions which have been included in the basal reader's teacher handbook.

Learning to Read in the Content Areas

Beginning with the third grade, children also learn to read in the "content areas" of the curriculum. This means that they learn how to read their social studies, science, and mathematics texts. Reading these texts requires special reading skills, since the vocabulary, sentence structure, and concepts presented are usually more difficult than the reading materials encountered in the basal readers. The content areas require particular reading skills: how to adjust the rate of reading to suit the difficulty of the content, how to scan material to locate pertinent information, how to put material in sequence, and how to use visual memory.

Teaching Library Media Center Skills

Most basal publishers intensify the teaching of library media center skills during the intermediate grades. The skills are usually incorporated in one or all of the following teaching areas: study skills, literary skills, extension activities, and enrichment activities. Publishers sometimes also incorporate library media center skills under a special section, in one basal series called the "Resource Center."[2] When publishers provide such material, it can be especially helpful to school library media specialists in that it recommends books and AV materials for the enhancement of the unit. The library media center skills section may also include the names and addresses of other resource agencies that can provide additional materials to enrich the teaching/learning process.

Meeting the Needs of Individual Readers

The teaching of reading in grades three to five would be fairly routine if children progressed at the same reading level. However, this definitely does not happen. Students may read at any level from second through eighth grade. Schools try to compensate for these differences through special reading programs that will meet the particular needs of individual readers. The most common method is to group children according to their reading abilities. This method requires that children leave their regular classroom and join others of the same reading ability in another classroom. This so-called "ability" grouping may also be achieved in each classroom; this is usually preferred when it is possible, since it saves time and much confusion.

To meet the needs of students who have severe reading problems, schools usually provide a reading resource room, headed by a reading specialist. The special diagnostic measures and teaching techniques provided by the reading specialist usually improve the reading abilities of the disabled readers.

Some school districts have also begun to use computer-assisted instruction for the reinforcement of skills that children have not mastered in their regular classroom lessons. Children assigned to computer-assisted instruction usually improve their reading skills. The novelty of the computer itself is sometimes conducive to challenge the less able learner into giving it another try. However, the novelty does wear off after some time, and learning may slacken at that point. Teachers have found the use of computers very helpful when they were programmed to keep track of each student's progress through a printout at the end of each lesson.

The use of computers for remedial instruction will probably become far more common when schools have adequate computer access as well as software appropriate for students' reading needs.

The Individualized Approach to Reading to Meet Individual Needs

Some schools have also instituted what is called an individualized approach to reading to help children of various reading abilities achieve their highest level of competency. Even though some schools have successfully implemented this approach at the first grade level, most schools wait until at least third grade to apply it. The reason for this is that the program is based on procedures too advanced for first graders: seeking, self-selection, and self-pacing.

In the individualized approach, children have the responsibility to select their own reading materials, particularly trade books, to read these books at their own speed, and thus to acquire all the reading skills in their own time and according to their own needs. Accomplishing all of these tasks is a great responsibility for students, and teachers are quick to recognize the need for certain modifications of the approach for particular students who cannot manage their time judiciously or select reading materials that will advance their reading skills. It should also be noted that even though the reading program is called individualized, it must basically adhere to all the reading objectives that have been established for a particular grade level.

Teachers usually initiate the individualized approach to reading by administering a reading interest inventory (*see* Appendixes B and C) as well as an informal reading inventory or survey (described in chapter 6). These will give the teacher better insight into the reading interests and abilities of the children.

Once the inventories have been administered and carefully examined, teachers develop a master list of books to be used in the reading program. Most teachers prefer to use paperbacks, which are less expensive and can be acquired in multiple copies. Once a master list has been completed and examined by children, the final selection of books to be used in the program will take place. Many teachers prefer to do this by asking students to vote on which books they wish to read. The books that receive the most votes are then purchased and read by students who gather in interest groups. For instance, if *Charlotte's Web* received ten votes, children who voted for this book would read it and meet in an interest group to discuss their common interest in it. Another book that might have received seven votes would be read by another interest group. Most individualized reading programs usually divide their students into at least four or five groups, depending on the size of the class and the number of different interests.

Managing the individualized approach. The teacher is totally responsible for the management of the individualized reading approach program. Many hours of careful preparation are needed to develop a program that will provide for the various reading needs of the students. To accomplish this goal, teachers must be knowledgeable in reading skills development. This means they must be especially familiar with the scope and sequence of reading skill development and how it applies to a certain grade level. The success of an individualized approach to reading, furthermore, demands that teachers have a very sound background in children's literature so that they can guide children to books that will meet their reading interests as well as reading needs. The books that students select must, after all, also serve as their basic reading texts.

To manage the individualized reading approach program, teachers usually design reading contracts that outline the skills that students must learn while reading a book. In schools where the individualized approach to reading is used in several grades, teachers sometimes pool their resources and share in the work of developing contracts which will adequately cover the teaching of the various reading skills. Many teachers also take advantage of the teacher guides that some paperback publishers make available with their most popular selections. These guides are most useful because they not only make suggestions for the teaching of literary skills but also include suggestions on how to use the book to teach decoding skills. The Dell Yearling Book Guides, prepared by Charles F. Reasoner, are a good example.[3]

The actual teaching of the reading lesson is accomplished through individual meetings between teacher and students or through group meetings. During the meeting teacher and student or students discuss and review the various skills that need to be learned. For instance, students might be asked to read certain parts of the book orally so that the teacher can appraise their oral reading abilities as well as their knowledge of word-attack skills. Comprehension skills and literary skills are usually introduced and reinforced through written work, which has been outlined in the student's contract.

Study skills and library media center skills are taught and reinforced through assignments that involve use of the school library media center. For example, the student might be asked to make a list of books by the author in addition to the one being studied. The student might be asked to collect biographical information on the author. As a follow-up or enrichment activity the student might go to the school library media center and research topics introduced in the book. In doing this investigative work, students, of course, are immediately expanding their reading skills in additional areas.

Evaluation of students' reading progress is usually achieved through oral examination as well as written examination.

How effective is the individualized approach? Schools that have tried the individualized approach to reading have, in most cases, endorsed it with great enthusiasm. The practicality of the program rests in its versatility and applicability to students who read below level as well as to students who are very gifted readers. One might not expect to see similarities between the reading needs of the reluctant reader and the gifted reader. However, similarities do exist, since both need special materials to satisfy their reading abilities and interests. Basal readers generally cannot meet these needs because they lack the versatility to reach the widely different reading abilities found among children.

Further evidence that the individualized approach works well is noted in a report by one school district which used it with 400 first graders in seventeen inner-city schools. In this case, a substantial increase in test scores was reported.[4] Based on this success, the school implemented the approach in the intermediate grades. Similar results were reported by another teacher who had to "smuggle" in an individualized reading program to help students who were headed towards reading failure.[5] It is important to note that both programs not only used books in their programs, but also included other materials such as newspapers, comic books, catalogs, pamphlets, and coupons to satisfy the reading interests of their students.

In summary, the teaching of reading in grades three to five demands that teachers look for teaching methods and materials which will captivate the attention of the readers and bolster their confidence so that they will become independent in their reading abilities.

Notes

1. Gill Schofer, "Reading Preferences of British and American Elementary Children," *Reading Improvement* 18:131 (Summer 1981).

2. Margaret Early et al., *HBJ Bookmark Reading Program* (New York: Harcourt, 1979).

3. Charles Reasoner, *Bringing Children and Books Together* (New York: Dell, 1979).

4. "Unorthodox Reading Programs that Work," *Instructor* 88: 112–113 (Sept. 1978).

5. Susan Ohanian, "Smuggling Reading into the Reading Program," *Learning* 10:44–47 (Nov. 1981).

8

Role of the School Library Media Specialist in Grades Three through Five

School library media specialists play a very important role in guiding children toward becoming independent readers. It is through their guidance that children may be liberated from the narrow confines of their classroom reading programs and led to the wider world of reading available to them in the school library media center.

The task of guiding children toward independence in reading as well as in school library media center use demands that school library media specialists understand the reading tasks that are specified for grades three through five. In addition, how readers in these grade levels respond to the reading tasks required of them is of very special concern to library media specialists.

From first-hand experience, library media specialists know all too well that reading guidance to students in these grade levels does not go as smoothly as desired, since children at this time are entering what may be characterized as their "topsy-turvy" years. Reading guidance, formerly accepted with a smile and even a courteous thank you, is often stubbornly ignored and even rejected now.

Some of this unusual behavior can be attributed to the great desire of children to gain independence from adults, to attain the freedom to make their own decisions. Some of their emotional upheavals are also brought about by anxieties children have about their physical development. Although children often feel a real need to share their fears with parents, all too often they are too embarrassed to do so. Adults too may find it difficult to discuss more sensitive topics with their children. Unable to deal with their frustrations, children sometimes vent their emotions through unexpected outbursts of anger. It also needs to be mentioned that while children adamantly seek independence from adults, they do not seek it from their peers and will gladly sacrifice it to become a member of an "in" group. If, therefore, one wished to describe the personality of children during these years, one might say they are unpredictable, vulnerable, yet capable of being lovable.

Considering the enigmatic behavior of the reader, it is very easy to understand why the role of the school library media specialist in the reading guidance process is not an easy one. However, the role can still be very productive if approached in a firm, patient, and loving manner.

A special hint. Two books dealing with child development, Havighurst's discussion of the developmental tasks of children of this age[1] and Erikson's description of childhood and its stages,[2] will give school library media specialists insight into the influences on children's well-being at these ages.

How to Promote the School Library Media Center Habit

Creating an inviting environment is fundamental to helping children become regular school library media center users. The library media center's environment must help readers feel that the materials there are useful for serious study, for browsing, or for enjoyable recreational reading. Its physical arrangement therefore must be such that children feel comfortable whether studying or browsing. Quiet corners with bean bags, cushions, or simple carpet squares are far more appealing to children than rows of tables and straight-back chairs. Study carrels, on the other hand, provide the privacy that serious students are looking for. A unique type of environment can be created for reluctant readers through displays that show off unusual reading materials such as magazines, comic books, and games. Even the use of a "What is it?" display that uses extraordinary objects of nature or manufacture will help catch the curiosities of children who need to become regular school library media center and public library users.

Providing an inviting reading environment is only the first step in getting everyone's attention. Library media specialists also need to provide materials that motivate children to read. To select the right materials, they again need to know what it is that children like to read. Reading interests must be solicited through surveys or group interviews with children. Library media specialists also need to reevaluate their collections. Collections that served students adequately a few years ago may be of little interest today. The influence that television and movies have in shaping children's reading interests cannot be overlooked. *Jaws, Star Wars,* and *E.T.* are only a few examples. Modern technology has also affected reading interests. Computer technology, robots, and electronic games also will undoubtedly have considerable impact on what children will want to read.

Authors may even influence the reading habits of children. This is particularly true of Judy Blume, who has captivated, or, one might say more accurately, "cult-ivated," the reading interests of children in grades four through six. Although Blume's writing lacks literary quality, and the manner in which her characters solve their problems is too simplistic, it is, nevertheless, in touch with the problems that today's children experience. In addition, her characters speak to the developmental needs which children experience at this age level and the problems children sometimes encounter because they are unable to share or resolve these needs with their parents.

In selecting books for children in these grades, library media specialists also should consider the many questions that children want answered. The most important questions pertain to getting along with themselves, their peers, and their parents. They also are looking for answers on how to develop appropriate masculine and feminine roles. There are other questions, as well. School library media specialists need to consider these questions very carefully so that their library media centers will reflect a good balance between books that preserve the delights of childhood and books that gently guide the reader toward adolescence.

IDEA: How to help children become independent library media center users. Children have a better chance of becoming independent readers if they know how to use the school library media center independently. To achieve this, library media specialists need to develop a library media center skills program that is both meaningful and useful.

The card catalog. Beginning with the third grade, children need to learn how to use the card catalog. For best results, lessons should be taught in conjunction with the reading activities in the classroom. Library media specialists and teachers should take the following steps:

1. Teacher and library media specialist review alphabetizing to ready children for understanding that the card catalog is arranged in alphabetical order.

2. Library media specialist reviews the arrangement of the card catalog by using giant author card and title card. At the same time, the library media specialist reviews the information given on the catalog cards: author, title, illustrator, publisher, copyright date, number of pages.
3. Teacher and library media specialist make up author slips that also note the title of each book. The first such lesson should include only fiction slips; later lessons may include nonfiction. The slips are placed in a box. At the time of the lesson, the children go to the box and each picks a slip.
4. Children go to the card catalog and find the catalog cards that match their author slips. They write down the call numbers for their slips.
5. The children go to the shelves and find their books. They check the books out. If their books are not on the shelves, students should draw another slip to have a second chance.

Subject cards. The use of subject cards should be taught as a separate lesson. The following steps may be followed:

1. Teacher and library media specialist select topics they would like the students to research in the library and prepare subject slips, which they place in the box.
2. The library media specialist reviews the subject card and its entries, again using a giant card, with the students.
3. The children draw topics out of the "magic box," look up one or two books on their topics in the card catalog, go to the shelves, find the books, and check them out.

A special hint. School library media centers which have card catalogs that are high and narrow may rearrange them so that a number of students can use them at once. For the elementary level, the card catalog should be no higher than four feet. Old, high card catalog cabinets can be lowered by simply cutting down the legs. If this is not possible, the card catalog may be divided by sections and placed on library tables for the lesson. By spreading out the card catalog this way many children will have ready access to it, and the dropping of drawers and fighting over use of the catalog will virtually disappear.

Basic reference books and their use. Children will also become more independent in their reading practices once they have learned how to use reference books. Beginning with the third grade, children are expected to learn how to use the following types of reference books: dictionaries (including specialized dictionaries such as author, geographical, and scientific), encyclopedias, almanacs (both state and world), and atlases. The primary emphasis in using reference tools is for the reader to learn the use of special parts of the book, such as table of contents, index, glossary, and pronunciation guide. Fourth and fifth graders are also expected to develop skills in using graphs: bar graphs, line graphs, pictographs, and time lines. Although children are provided with examples of reference books and the terms for their parts in the basal readers, children usually find the examples difficult to follow unless they have access to a real dictionary, atlas, topographical map, and books that use graphs. Library media specialists can, therefore, improve the learning of these skills by setting up a reference skill learning center in the school library media center or in the classroom.

Almanacs. Library media specialists should review with children the use of almanacs before sending them to the learning center. For example, to review the *World Almanac*, they may direct children's attention to the location and use of the general index and to some of the special sections of the almanac, such as:

Special dates in U.S. history
Sports records
Population figures.

After the review lesson, each child should be scheduled for use of the learning center to complete work sheets on the use of the almanac. The learning center should have at least four or five learning stations, each supplied with:

A copy of the almanac
Ten questions, typed and laminated (each station should have a different set of questions)
An answer sheet (answers to be filled in or circled)
A master self-check answer sheet to conserve the library media specialist's time. Students get this from the library media specialist upon completion of the assignment.

Specialized dictionaries and reference books. Fourth and fifth graders are ready to be introduced to specialized dictionaries and other reference books, such as *Webster's Biographical Dictionary*, *Webster's New Geographical Dictionary*, *Compton's Dictionary of Natural Science*, *Mathematics Illustrated Dictionary*, *American Book of Days*, and *Famous First Facts*.

These reference tools should be introduced one or two at a time by the library media specialist during regular media center periods. The introductions will be most effective if the library media specialist has made up a list of questions to be used during each introduction. For instance, for the *American Book of Days*, children might be asked, "What happens on July 19th that will make you hungry?" (National Cherry Festival), and "What happens on October 5th that will make you less fearful of going to the hospital?" (Ether Day). After the library media specialist has introduced these specialized reference books, children should complete work sheets, each containing ten to fifteen questions, at the learning center. The work sheets should be self-checking.

To encourage students to become independent readers, library media specialists may wish to conclude the unit by asking them to submit a list of questions (with answers and sources) to be used with other students.

IDEA: Sustained Silent Reading during the school day. Children only become independent readers when they are allowed ample time to read the books they want to read. To accomplish this, school library media specialists can push for a Sustained Silent Reading (SSR), or Drop Everything and Read (DEAR), period in their schools. These SSR or DEAR periods may be either daily or weekly. The minimum length of a period should be 15 minutes if it is scheduled daily, 30 minutes if weekly.

It is important that everyone in the school become involved in this program. This definitely includes the principal. It might also include the cafeteria workers, custodians, and other people the school employs. It is also very important that children be allowed to read what they want. This means that they may read their comic books, newspapers, magazines, pamphlets, catalogs, or coupons— anything in print.

SSR and DEAR periods should be promoted throughout the school by a bulletin board. Children should be encouraged to advertise their reading likes or dislikes on this board. Teachers and principals should also make an extra effort to take advantage of the bulletin board. They might enjoy writing reviews in the form of "Dear Ann Landers" letters and responses to encourage children to reach for the books. For example,

Dear Ann,

I have been given a runt pig and need your help in finding a diet that will make it grow.

Sincerely,
A desperate principal

Dear Principal:

Read the book *Charlotte's Web* to help you with your problems. It is waiting for you in your library media center.

A special hint. Some special reading materials needed for the SSR program in the classrooms can be supplied through the school library media center. Outdated magazines, which are sometimes donated to the library, can be put to good use. For instance, old copies of *Reader's Digest* cut up to provide single story sections can be stapled and given to the teacher in a little box for distribution to problem readers.

Teachers needing materials for students who do not have the patience to read an entire book can be given chapters cut from books that are damaged beyond repair. The author and title of the book from which the chapter was taken should be noted somewhere. A secret code might even be used to encourage children to guess the title of the book. Free materials such as recipe books, store catalogs, and repair manuals may also be given to classroom teachers who have problem readers.

Special paperbacks, such as those in the "Choose Your Own Adventure" series published by Bantam may also be purchased for the SSR program. If additional money is available, copies of puzzle books, riddle books, and joke books may also be acquired for students who are just getting into the reading habit.

School districts with very limited library resources may wish to investigate the use of the RIF (Reading Is Fundamental) program. The program does require a group of select volunteers who are willing to go out and solicit financial help from the community at large. Information about the program may be obtained from: Reading Is Fundamental, Washington, D.C. 20002.

IDEA: Use Children's Choices to initiate a local Children's Choices program. Every year thousands of children from around the country have the opportunity to name the current children's books they believe are the best in a program sponsored by the International Reading Association and the Children's Book Council Joint Committee. The results of the survey are published annually in the October issue of *The Reading Teacher.* Even though not every child can be part of this program, school library media specialists can use the list to select books that appeal to children.

To promote a local Children's Choices program, school library media specialists may:

1. Develop a slogan to get children's attention that something special is about to happen in the school library media center, such as "You be the judge! Do you think these books are really the best?" "Would these be your choices? Come in and find out." The slogan might be posted in the school as well as the library.
2. Tell children all about Children's Choices during a regular library media center period.
3. Ask children to select books from the Children's Choices list. Have each reader respond to the chosen book by completing a form, such as,

Author: _____

Title: _____

I would have selected this book. Yes _____ No _____

Yes, because _____

No, because _____

Teachers may wish to use this form to satisfy the requirement of a book report.

IDEA: The biggest read-in ever. Children's Book Week is the special time of year when everyone in the school should stretch their reading to the limit. To accomplish this, library media specialists might establish a read-in, with specific goals. One such goal might be the number of pages read during this special week. For instance, the reading goal might be 10,000 pages (this would depend on the size of the school). Library media specialists should also develop specific guidelines. These guidelines need to include the following information:

Day and hour when read-in begins and ends

Place or places of read-in (it should probably only take place in the school under the supervision of library media specialists and teachers)

What materials count (the read-in might be limited to books)

Place and time when scores are recorded

Place where chart recording progress will be posted.

A well-known personality of the community might be asked to participate in the read-in and to be the official score keeper. Local media should also be notified so that they can report the progress of the read-in throughout the week.

Notes

1. Robert James Havighurst, *Developmental Tasks and Education*, 3d ed. (New York: Longman, 1979).

2. Erik H. Erikson, *Childhood and Society*, 2d ed. (New York: W.W. Norton, 1963).

9

How to Prepare a Successful Workshop

The presentation of workshops is of utmost importance in that it provides library media specialists with the great opportunity to promote the school library media center as the heart of the school from which and to which all learning should flow. It also affords them the opportunity to let their fellow teachers know that they have the professional expertise to provide educational leadership and present innovative teaching and learning ideas.

Planning and presenting a workshop can be a very successful experience if school library media specialists follow some of the rules listed below during the preliminary planning stages.

Rule no. 1: *Make it short!* Workshops of 40 to 60 minutes will be far more effective than presentations that last several hours. Shorter workshops can also be squeezed more easily into busy schedules.

Rule no. 2: *Plan manageable workshops!* Workshops should be manageable for you as well as for the participants. Please remember, it is the participants who will ultimately have to carry out the ideas in the classrooms.

Rule no. 3: *Limit equipment and materials!* Never overwhelm your audience with too much equipment or too many materials. Likewise, don't overwhelm yourself with too many items and details to handle. Using one piece of equipment to demonstrate teaching/learning ideas will be far more effective than using too many pieces of AV and too many materials.

Rule no. 4: *Treat your audience with professional courtesy!* Present your teaching/learning ideas in such a manner that your participants will feel involved and their viewpoints valued.[1]

Rule no. 5: *Consider and research the needs of each grade level!* This rule is of utmost importance since certain grade levels have their own teaching and learning needs. For instance, kindergarten and first grade teachers need to know that the school library media center not only welcomes children who are just beginning to learn to read, but that the library media center has materials which are appropriate for these children. Second and third grade teachers, on the other hand, need to know that the school library media center can provide reading challenges for children who are advanced readers as well as those who are still trying to catch up. Fourth and fifth grade teachers need to be informed how library media specialists can become team members in teaching children to become independent readers and independent library media center users.

Developing the workshop. With the foregoing rules in mind, proceed with the steps that follow to develop a memorable in-service workshop. Its success is virtually assured!

1. Select a topic that you really like.
2. Define the topic (for example, if Newbery books are a topic you really like, a workshop might be about "How to Get Fourth and Fifth Graders into the 'Newbery' Habit").
3. Make a plan of how you are going to present the topic to your audience. The best method is the regular lesson plan approach (see sample lesson plan).
4. Determine whether you have adequate materials to present your topic.
5. Decide which AV equipment is most suitable for your presentation.
6. Discuss the workshop with your principal or supervisor.
7. Schedule your workshop.
8. Make short attractive invitations announcing your workshop. Place invitations in teachers' mailboxes.
9. Get your library media center ready for your audience.
10. Plan simple refreshments.
11. Get your enthusiasm up. Finalize your plans.
12. Do it! Smile! Let your audience know you are enjoying it! SUCCESS!

Sample Lesson Plan

Topic: How to get children into the "Newbery" habit.

Behavioral objectives: Upon completion of this workshop, every participant will be able to:

1. Select a Newbery book to read aloud to students.
2. Motivate children to read Newbery books by using a thematic approach, such as

    Courageous children in Newbery books
    Horses in Newbery books
    Special animals in Newbery books
    Science fiction in Newbery books.

3. Motivate children to report on Newbery books using either oral, written, or AV book report method.

Materials needed:

1. List of Newbery award winners
2. Display of Newbery books according to themes to be used
3. Sample book reports demonstrating oral, written, and AV methods
4. Overhead projector

Procedure:

1. Open workshop by reading exciting and humorous excerpt from one Newbery book.
2. Hand out Newbery list.
3. Introduce audience to recurring themes in Newbery books.
4. Show audience how they can get children to read Newbery books by using thematic approach.
5. Show audience examples of oral, written, and AV book reports.
6. Allow time for questions.

Evaluation: At the end of the workshop every participant will:

1. Check out at least one Newbery book
2. Read a Newbery book to his or her students
3. Discuss with students the various themes found in Newbery books
4. Ask children to come to the library to begin their Newbery habit.

An easy evaluation form. The following short evaluation form may be handed out at the end of the workshop:

I found the workshop useful   Yes _____ No _____
I would like to attend another workshop on the following topic: _____

The length of the workshop was appropriate for the topic   Yes _____
No _____
I felt my opinions were valued   Yes _____ No _____

Interlibrary Cooperation for Presenting Workshops

Library media specialists in districts with more than one elementary school may pool their resources by sharing in the task of presenting workshops. For instance, if a workshop is prepared for a certain grade level in one school, the same workshop should be presented in another school. The library media specialist in that school might reciprocate by presenting a workshop on a special topic for the partner school. Planning workshops in this cooperative manner will not only save time but will also add new life to the school library media center's programs. To set this cooperative arrangement in motion, library media specialists may wish to plan their workshops at the beginning of the school year.

Where to Get Those Super-duper Workshop Ideas

Your first source of ideas is your teachers. Listen to their recommendations and also to their complaints. Write down some of their suggestions and look into the possibility of developing a workshop around their requests.

Next, check your professional journals for successful teaching ideas. Topics like "Apple-ations on a Theme,"[2] and "The Science of Goldfish,"[3] are only two examples of ideas that can be adapted for workshop presentations. Review ideas you learned at a conference and adapt them to your own school's needs.

Finally, use your very own ideas: these will probably produce the very best workshops and turn out to be your most successful.

Notes

1. Lea-Ruth C. Wilkens, "Involvement in the Educational Program Part 1: You Can Be Accountable," *School Library Journal* 23:43 (Dec. 1976).

2. Dorothy Needham, "Apple-ations on a Theme," *Teacher* 96:110–20 (Oct. 1978).

3. Alan J. McCormack, "The Science of Goldfish," *Instructor* 88:125–32 (Mar. 1979).

10

The Disabled Reader (The Reader with a Broken Wing)

A disabled reader, the "flyer with a broken wing," is a child who, after having had adequate reading instruction, fails to perform at the reading level expected from comparisons with other children of the same age and intelligence. Disabled readers, because of their reading disabilities, usually experience mild to severe learning problems in other subject areas, as well.

Children become disabled readers because of one or more disabling factors, usually classified under three major categories: intellectual, physical, and emotional. Other factors, not belonging to these categories, may also interfere with a child's ability to perform the required reading skills, such as lack of motivation, poor reading instruction, lack of parental support, cultural and language differences. Another special category is dyslexia. Diagnosis of reading problems must, therefore, be based on careful examination of a variety of factors to provide an adequate profile of the causes that may be preventing a student from becoming a successful reader.

Identification of the Disabled Reader

Identification of the disabled reader usually begins right in the classroom. The diagnosis is made by the classroom teacher who makes note of the special difficulties that the reader is experiencing while performing various reading tasks. If the problems seem to be minor, teachers in most cases try to help students overcome their difficulties by initiating special reinforcement lessons.

Problems of a more severe nature require that teachers try to review the child's previous educational background and reading tests, if available. For example, has the child ever failed to be promoted? If so, was the promotion withheld because of reading difficulties? How often has the child changed schools? Does the child have a medical history that might influence his or her reading abilities or reading scores? In what subjects or classes has the reader failed? Once the teacher has found the answers to these questions, a more personalized remedial reading plan can be structured.

Teachers who determine a possible correlation between reading difficulties and either home environment or health problems of the reader usually try to arrange for a parent-teacher conference in order to discuss how the problems may be remedied. It is during these conferences that teachers sometimes can verify whether the reading problems are indeed related to a home environment that negatively influences the child's reading behavior and attitude. Should it be discovered that parents have reading expectations that are beyond the reader's ability, the teacher may suggest that parents set more realistic goals. Or, if it is discovered that parents rarely read to or with their children, the teacher may suggest this practice to strengthen the reader's reading skills and attitude.

In instances where readers make no progress after all of the foregoing measures have been implemented, teachers may recommend that children undergo additional diagnostic testing by a reading specialist or a reading diagnostician. The results of these tests may provide additional information which will be used to move toward a decision on whether a reader should be placed in a remedial reading classroom or clinic, or whether additional professional help is needed to diagnose the causes of the interference with the student's ability to read at expected level.

Diagnosis of Disabling Factors

Intellectual. Although intelligence of the disabled reader is usually among the first factors to be checked, the findings are also interpreted with extreme caution since intelligence tests are by no means foolproof. To verify the intellectual ability of a disabled reader it is very important that the reader be given an individual intelligence test instead of one which is administered to a group of children. Tests which are usually recommended for this diagnostic procedure are the Wechsler Intelligence Scale for Children, Revised (WISC-R), the Stanford-Binet Intelligence Scale, or the Peabody Picture Vocabulary Test. Because of the special nature of these tests, it is necessary that they be administered by clinicians who have special training in the area of testing. The initial test result should also be validated by administering a second, or even a third, test.

Additional testing is recommended because not all intelligence tests are designed to take into consideration the cultural background of the disabled reader. It is known that language and cultural differences may affect both a student's test score (not his or her intelligence) and reading achievement. It is very important that such factors be taken into account with children whose backgrounds dispose them to low intelligence scores and poor reading achievement scores. These children should not be relegated to reading groups that are aimed at children of genuinely low intelligence, since the reading groups for the latter use different methods and work at different paces than the remedial classes for children whose main difficulty is a cultural or language difference.

Teachers who discover students with relatively high intelligence scores reading well below their anticipated level might recommend that these children undergo additional diagnostic testing to search out the factors that could be causing their reading problems. The WISC-R and Stanford-Binet tests mentioned earlier are highly regarded tests that are individually administered to help determine the mental ability of both able and disabled readers. Clinicians and reading specialists frequently refer to the score obtained by either test as an I.Q. and may use it to help estimate the level at which a child should be able to read. For instance, it is generally recognized that children with intelligence scores below 100, particularly in the 75 to 90 range, usually have greater reading difficulties than children who have scores of 100 and up. Although children with an intelligence score of 75 may eventually learn to read, it will take them longer than it will children with scores of 100 and above. Since the intelligence score seems to be a fairly accurate indicator of a child's rate of learning, it is used to estimate his or her reading potential by means of the following formula:

$$\text{Reading Expectancy} = \frac{\text{I.Q.} + (100 \times \text{years of reading instruction})}{100}$$

A child with an I.Q. of 100 should, therefore, be able to read at the second grade level at the end of the first grade.[1] Similarly, a second grader with an I.Q. of 125 should be able to read at the 3.25 grade level at the end of the second grade. A second grader with an I.Q. of 90 should, however, only be able to read at the 2.9 level at the end of second grade, so an achievement score of 2.9 does not indicate any specific disability with regard to reading, only a slightly slower general learning ability.

The size of the discrepancy between reading expectancy and reading achievement required before reading disability is diagnosed increases with age of the child. For a first grader, a discrepancy of half a year is considered to be evidence of reading disability,[2] but for a fourth grader, the discrepancy must be around one year.[3]

Finally, it should be remembered that intelligence scores represent only one diagnostic measure of why children can or cannot read. Every child, regardless of his or her intellectual ability, should be given the opportunity to undergo other diagnostic testing to discover if other factors are interfering with reading ability. When evaluating the test results, the teacher or diagnostician should always ask, "Could the test results be incorrect?" "How did the child feel when the test was administered?" "Was there a language or a cultural problem?" and "Does the child experience any physical and emotional problems?"

Vision. The reading process requires that children have good visual acuity or clearness of vision in order to be successful readers. Children, for instance, who are afflicted with farsightedness (hyperopia) may have excellent vision of materials written on a chalkboard 15 to 20 feet away but are unable to easily read the print on the pages of a book held in their hands or placed on a desk. Children who experience great difficulty reading fine print may eventually become reluctant readers or even disabled in their reading practices. Farsightedness may be a less apparent problem in the first and second grades because so much of the reading material is printed in large letters, but it can become a serious problem in the intermediate grades when children are confronted with textbooks printed in considerably smaller typefaces. Farsighted children may become irritable, nervous, and emotionally upset. They may also complain of headaches, dizziness, and upset stomachs. When watching these readers, one sometimes observes that they are constantly rubbing their eyes, tilting their heads, or holding their books too close to their eyes.

While children may put up with the discomforts brought about by farsightedness for a while, they become more reluctant to do so as reading demands increase. Recent research has indicated that children of higher intelligence are less tolerant of this situation than slower children who will put up with the discomforts even though doing so may not bring about any more desirable reading results. Although farsightedness may be corrected easily, it is too often undetected because of inadequate vision screening. This is particularly true when only the Snellen chart, which indicates only what a person can see at a distance of twenty feet, is used. It is suggested, therefore, that children who exhibit any of the signs of farsightedness be referred to the school nurse or reading specialist for additional vision screening. The instrument that might be used to test for farsightedness is either the Ortho-Rater (Bausch and Lomb) or the Telebinocular (Keystone).

Although nearsightedness (myopia) is far less significant as far as reading difficulties are concerned, it may still be a contributing factor in the reading disabling process. This is particularly true if the reader is required to copy or read instructions from the chalkboard located at the far end of the classroom. Readers who cannot read the instructions listed on the board will not be able to complete their assignments correctly. Consequently, they may receive lower grades, perhaps leading to a loss in self-confidence and finally a loss of reading interest.

Children in kindergarten and first grade who experience reading disabilities should also be checked for lazy-eye blindness (amblyopia). Children with lazy-eye blindness have eyes that do not work together. Our two eyes must converge on an object in order for us to see it clearly, and children who cannot achieve this clear vision might actually find reading a very painful process, ultimately refusing to participate in the reading lessons. Therefore, children who seem to have problems with lazy-eye blindness should be referred to the school nurse or reading specialist immediately for additional testing and possible treatment. It is also recommended that all children should be checked for lazy-eye blindness before they enter kindergarten to prevent any early reading problems from becoming major disabling factors in the future.

Children also need to be checked for color recognition (color blindness). Many reading tasks require that children identify objects by colors presented to them in picture clues. Children who are color blind will not be able to determine colors correctly and will fail to complete the assignment as called for.

The reading process also requires that readers have ocular motility. Ocular motility means that readers must be able to move their eyes in rhythmic movements, also called saccadic movements, from left to right and from line to line. The stops that the eyes make during saccadic movements are called fixations. It is during the fixation that the reader perceives a printed symbol or symbols. The number of symbols that a reader perceives during a fixation is referred to as perception span. Readers who do not have the ability to move their eyes in the saccadic movements will experience reading problems such as rereading words and skipping lines. How the eyes move can be photographed by the Reading Eye Camera, and can also be observed through the use of the Tele-binocular.

Visual perception. The term "visual perception" extends beyond the immediate boundaries of vision already described and includes such functions as language ability, motor coordination, and intelligence. How perception is developed within the young has been carefully investigated by Jean Piaget, the renowned child psychologist. Those who are familiar with the theories that Piaget proposed in his research realize the complexity of his studies. What can be gleaned from sources that have interpreted some of Piaget's theories is that the development of children's perception is related to the environmental experiences to which they are exposed. In the earliest stages environmental experiences promote sensory motor development, eventually leading to the ability to perceive space, direction, width, size, and shape. The very young child begins to learn these concepts through concrete experiences involving much touching and doing. The result of these very concrete experiences should facilitate the perception of constancy of form and size. As children mature, so should their abilities of perception. By age nine, the child should have matured enough to be able to function on the abstract level. In terms of reading, this means that the child has the ability to process symbols such as words, which, when placed in arbitrary positions, become phrases.

Inability to process symbols (visual perceptual problems) can lead to reading disabilities. However, this type of disability can be diagnosed by using Criterion Phrase Tests or the Reading Eye Camera.

Hearing. Poor hearing ability may be another contributor to becoming a disabled reader as a child. Good hearing (auditory acuity) is of great importance for all reading tasks. It is particularly important if children are taught reading using the phonetic method, which requires the reader to discriminate between various sounds. For example, readers need to hear the differences in consonant sounds as they appear in the initial position—/b/ in *b*at and /p/ in *p*at; medial (middle) positon—/m/ in ca*m*e and /n/ in ca*n*e; and end position—/b/ in ca*b* and /p/ in ca*p*. They must also have the auditory acuity needed to differentiate among the various long and short vowel sounds—/a/ in *a*pricot, *a*pple, s*a*w, and c*a*r. Children who experience hearing problems usually find the phonetic approach to teaching reading very difficult to follow. The various sound nuances that must be audible within the phonetic reading process usually are quite incomprehensible to them. Because their inability to differentiate among the various sounds is so frustrating, they usually become reluctant participants in the daily reading lesson.

One clue to hearing problems is the inattentiveness of readers during reading lessons. Teachers may note a hearing impaired child turning one ear to or leaning toward the speaker. The same child may also ask the speaker to repeat instructions several times. Children with hearing problems sometimes also exhibit poor speech habits in that they speak and read in a monotone and habitually leave off endings when speaking and reading.

It should also be noted that not all hearing problems are physical in nature. Some children with no physical hearing problems may exhibit symptoms similar to those who actually have physical hearing loss. Children who lack listening skills or who seem to be unable to memorize sounds (auditory memory) are usually referred to as "lazy" listeners. They are termed "lazy" since they have not learned to listen carefully and internalize the sounds they hear. Lazy listening habits are frequently found among children who have not been introduced to many listening activities during their preschool years. The problem itself can be remedied through instruction by the classroom teacher or reading specialist according to special methods.

General health. Learning to read can be a very strenuous mental activity, which requires that students be in good health to keep up with the demands of the daily reading routines. Children who are frequently ill and miss many days in the classroom because of poor health usually find it difficult to expend the effort that learning to read demands. Even children who come to class every day may lack the physical stamina to be active participants in the reading program. Children who fall into this category often complain of headaches, nausea, stomach pains, and dizziness. Although poor health may be caused by various bodily malfunctions, including painful glandular defects, it may also be caused by poor dietary habits and malnutrition. Even the lack of sleep cannot be overlooked as a cause for a child's not feeling well enough to actively participate in the daily reading lesson. The influence of drugs on reading behavior is yet another factor that must be considered. Children who are taking special medication for certain chronic illnesses or to regulate hyperactivity need to be carefully monitored to be sure such drugs do not influence their behavior and their ability to learn during the regular school day. The reader's health, therefore, needs to be carefully observed if he or she shows signs of poor reading ability.

Emotional condition. Children who feel good about themselves and have a certain amount of self-confidence usually experience fewer reading problems than children who have poor self-images and little confidence in their ability to become good readers. Emotional problems that children may experience can be related to various influences. The two most common sources of these problems are the school and the home.

Emotional problems may arise in the classroom because the teacher has failed to create a reading environment that helps children feel positive about their reading abilities. Teachers, for instance, who are unable to adjust their teaching styles to fit some of the learning styles of children sometimes inadvertently cause emotional pressures that may eventually lead to reading disabilities. Emotional problems can also occur if children fail to get along with their peers in the reading group to which they have been assigned. In such situations, students may be paying more attention to ways and means of upsetting other students than to what the teacher is saying and doing. Some emotional problems may also be traced to a child's inability to adjust to a new school. This is a very real problem in this day when families are often on the move. Changing schools and changing friends can cause serious emotional problems for children who find it difficult to make new friends with whom they can share their childhood joys and fears.

Home environments also influence how readers feel about themselves as well as how they feel about the importance of learning to read. Parents who are nurturing their children's reading endeavors through positive comments and many read-aloud experiences can do much to help readers develop positive attitudes toward the reading process. Children's attitudes can, furthermore, be bolstered when parents are willing to temper their reading expectations with the abilities that their children actually have at a particular stage of development. Home environments that overemphasize superior performance sometimes create stress problems that lead to emotional problems and produce a disabled reader. Sound emotional conditions in the reader are created when home and school form a partnership and create environments which stimulate and encourage readers to perform to their highest potential.

Other factors. Reading environments that take a very positive stance toward each reader's ability encourage reading success.

This means that each child must be measured first of all against his or her own ability. Some children may become disabled readers because teachers neglect to consider this factor and set their expectations too high or too low. The reading environment can also be placed in jeopardy when teachers exhibit a negative attitude toward their students' reading ability and share this attitude with others in the presence of their students. Students who are constantly exposed to such remarks as, "My students are the low group. They never will amount to much," cannot but help to feel inferior and achieve accordingly. Teachers, therefore, need to watch their attitudes to prevent and circumvent poor performance in their students.

Another factor that can seriously endanger the reading performance of children is poor teacher preparation. Teachers who are placed in elementary classrooms without a strong reading background sometimes lack the skills to meet the various reading needs of their students. Teachers, for instance, who feel insecure in teaching the fundamentals of phonics will be ill prepared to help those students who are struggling with the various sound nuances and rules of phonics. Reading teachers need to be extremely knowledgeable and flexible in their teaching techniques in order to satisfy the various learning needs and learning styles of the children assigned to their classrooms. Teachers who are unable or unwilling to search for additional materials to saturate the reading thirst of very gifted students may inadvertently stunt their reading growth. Teachers who neglect to look for simplified materials to help slower learners overcome reading fears may harm the slower learners, as well.

The textbook used for reading instruction may be another factor in whether children approach reading with enthusiasm or with trepidation. Reading texts that are made up of lackluster stories and accompanied by artless illustrations may stifle readers' enthusiasm for the reading lesson. For serious learning to take place readers need to approach the text with a good measure of excitement as well as a willingness to stick with it even though reading may become progressively more difficult.

A lack of reading readiness by first grade students is another factor that can affect how well children are able to perform the required reading tasks. Children who have not attended preschool or kindergarten where they might have been introduced to the readiness skills may run a greater risk of becoming disabled readers than children who possess these skills.

Dyslexia. The term *dyslexia* in its broadest sense means inability to read. Dyslexic readers may exhibit one or more of the following problems during reading lessons. They perform poorly during phonic skills lessons because they lack auditory memory. They reverse letters while reading orally because of visual memory and visual discrimination problems. Instead of reading /b/ as in /boat/, they read /d/ as in /doat/. Some dyslexic readers may even reverse entire words, for example, reading /saw/ for /was/. These reversal patterns are usually also carried over into spelling and handwriting lessons. Some dyslexic readers even attempt to read from right to left and also write from right to left. Because many dyslexic readers also experience great difficulties with hand-eye coordination they frequently lose their place during reading lessons. Their overall behavior may be termed clumsy. Some dyslexic children also display short attention spans as well as very distractive behaviors. This trait can, of course, be directly related to their great frustrations in trying to survive in a reading environment that is not compatible with their abilities.

Whether this inability to read is brought about by one cause or multiple causes has not been clearly defined. At present several theories exist. For example, single-factor theorists propose that the dyslexic reader might have a neurological dysfunction in visuospatial processing.[4] Multiple-factor theorists propose that the reader might have deficiencies in both auditory and visual spheres.[5] A third theory suggests that "four basic processes are consistently implicated as possible areas of difficulty: visual perception, intersensory integration, temporal ordering, and verbal processing.[6] Spache, in his book *Diagnosing and Correcting Reading Disabilities*, makes another important observation in that he suggests that the "presence of brain damage or suspected brain damage as a basic component of dyslexia is both anatomically, neurologically, and hereditarily untenable."[7] Other sources seem to agree with Spache in that dyslexic readers usually do have normal if not above normal intelligence.

Children who are diagnosed as being dyslexic are usually assigned to a special reading teacher who can apply reading methods and reading materials which are more suitable for these children. Children who test out as severely dyslexic may receive additional remedial help from a reading clinic which has the staff and facilities not usually available at the school level.

The Helping Role of the Library Media Specialist

School library media specialists, as partners of the teaching team, need to be knowledgeable of the factors that cause children to become disabled readers. They need to apply this special knowledge when they work with teachers as well as when they work with disabled readers. Their role in helping disabled readers is not one of diagnostician but of remediation specialist. They can be of greatest service to disabled readers by:

Consulting with teachers to select appropriate print and non-print materials for the disabled reader

Working with reading diagnosticians and special reading teachers to select appropriate reading materials for the special reading clinic or reading center

Working with children to select materials suitable for their special reading needs

Meeting with parents and the community at large to develop special reading programs for the disabled reader

Recruiting special volunteers to work with disabled readers

Setting up special reading areas for disabled readers

Guiding the school and community toward reading programs which might prevent children from becoming disabled readers

Alerting teachers to current research dealing with new teaching methods as well as materials appropriate for the disabled reader.

Although suggestions have been made throughout the book on how library media specialists can help disabled readers, sometimes also called "slower" readers or "reluctant readers," some additional recommendations are made at this point to help them locate the special resources needed for these special children.

To keep up to date on current materials appropriate and helpful for these readers library media specialists need regularly to review *Booklist*, published by the American Library Association. Books suitable for children with reading difficulties are reviewed under the heading "Easy Reading." Each review of this kind provides an interest level (IL) as well as reading level (RL) which has been determined using the Fry Graph.

The Reading Teacher, published by the International Reading Association for the members of IRA and others concerned with reading, is another journal which should be consulted regularly for bibliographies as well as informative articles on how to select materials for disabled readers. Articles such as "A Successful Program for First Grade Remedial Reading Instruction,"[8] will be invaluable in formulating plans to help students with reading problems. The section called "Interchange" and "Clip Sheet" should also be consulted on a regular basis for teaching ideas and book suggestions to satisfy the special needs of children with reading difficulties.

Another journal which should be checked regularly is *Language Arts*, published by the National Council of Teachers of English. Articles such as "A Writing Program for Poor Readers and Writers and the Rest of the Class Too"[9] present invaluable ideas for both teachers and library media specialists who are looking for innovative teaching and learning ideas for their students. Special reports such as "Motivating Reluctant Readers: A Gentle Push,"[10] which appeared under the regular ERIC/RCS section in this journal, should not be overlooked when reviewing the journal for special learning and teaching ideas.

Childhood Education, published by the Association for Childhood Education International is another journal which contains many articles and practical suggestions on how to help children with special reading needs. Not to be missed are such special features as "Educating Children with Special Needs."[11] This article reviewed films which could be used for in-service workshops for both teachers and parents.

Teaching Exceptional Children and *Exceptional Children*, two journals published by the Council for Exceptional Children, should also be consulted for special articles and resources on how to help children who are experiencing special reading problems.

Finally, to truly understand the problems of teaching a dyslexic child, teachers, school library media specialists, and parents need to read Louise Clarke's very special story of her own son's struggle with the problem entitled *Can't Read, Can't Write, Can't Talk Too Good Either.*"[12]

Notes

1. Guy L. Bond and others, *Reading Difficulties: Their Diagnosis and Correction*, 4th ed. (Englewood Cliffs, N.J.: Prentice-Hall, 1979), p. 62.

2. Ibid., p. 63.

3. Ibid., p. 64.

4. Arthur L. Benton and David Pearl, eds., *Dyslexia: An Appraisal of Current Knowledge* (New York: Oxford Univ. Pr., 1978), p. 70.

5. Ibid., p. 70.

6. Ibid., p. 70.

7. George D. Spache, *Diagnosing and Correcting Reading Disabilities*, 2nd ed. (Boston: Allyn, 1981), p. 358.

8. Barbara A. Mathews and Jane B. Seibert, "A Successful Program for First Grade Remedial Reading Instruction," *The Reading Teacher* 37: 408–9 (Jan. 1983).

9. Irene Gaskins, "A Writing Program for Poor Readers and Writers and the Rest of the Class, Too," *Langugae Arts* 59:854–61 (Dec. 1982).

10. Hilary Taylor Holbrook, "Motivating Reluctant Readers: A Gentle Push," *Language Arts* 59:385–89 (Apr. 1982).

11. E. Anne Eddowes, "Educating Children with Special Needs," *Childhood Education* 59:206–8 (Jan./Feb. 1983).

12. Louise Clarke, *Can't Read, Can't Write, Can't Talk Too Good Either* (Baltimore: Penguin, 1973).

Appendix A

Letter to Parents

Dear Parent,

Have you read to your children today? If you have, then you have done your part in helping your children become better readers. If you have been unaware of how important it is to share books with your children, you may be pleased to know that it is never too late to begin the habit of taking ten or fifteen minutes out of your busy schedule to share a bedtime story with your children.

We have attached a list of books to help you get started in reading aloud to your children in your home. These books are available to you either through your local bookstore, the public library, or your children's very own school library media center.

Come and see us soon to select your read-aloud books so that you and your children can participate in and enjoy one of the best reading experiences of your lives.

Sincerely,

Estimados padres,

¿Han leído algo a sus hijos hoy? Si ha sido así—Uds han hecho su parte al ayudar a sus hijos a ser mejores lectores. Si han sido Uds. algo negligentes en compartir la lectura de algunos libros con sus hijos, les agradará saber que nunca es demasiado tarde para comenzar el buen hábito de tomar diez o quince minutos de vuestro díapara compartir con sus hijos una historia o un cuento antes de que se duerman.

Estamos incluyendo una lista de libros que Uds. pueden utilizar favorablemente para principiar en casa la costumbre de leer en voz alta. Tales libros están a vuestra disposición a través de la libreria local, la biblioteca pública, o la biblioteca de la propia escuela.

Vengan pronto para seleccionar los libros que Uds. quisieran leerles en voz alta, y así sus niños no perderán en sus vidas la maravillosa experiencia que proporciona la lectura.

Sinceramente,

Reading Interest Survey for Grades One and Two

Questions should be read to children.

1. Do you like to listen to dog stories?   Yes ___   No ___
2. Do you like to listen to horse stories?   Yes ___   No ___
3. Do you like to listen to ghost stories?   Yes ___   No ___
4. Do you like to listen to stories about boys and girls like you?   Yes ___   No ___
5. Do you like to listen to stories about boys and girls who live in the city?   Yes ___   No ___
6. Do you like to listen to stories about farm animals?   Yes ___   No ___
7. Do you like to listen to "make believe" stories such as "Cinderella"?   Yes ___   No ___
8. My mother or father reads to me every day.   Yes ___   No ___
9. My mother or father reads to me sometimes.   Yes ___   No ___
10. I like to have someone read to me before I go to bed.   Yes ___   No ___
11. I watch television every evening before I go to bed.   Yes ___   No ___
12. I have received a book as a birthday gift.   Yes ___   No ___

Boy ___ Girl ___
Grade _____

Reading Interest Survey for Intermediate Grades

1. Did you read a book or magazine today?   Yes ___   No ___
2. Do you read because you want to get good grades?   Yes ___   No ___
3. Do you read because you think reading is great?   Yes ___   No ___
4. Do you like to read comic books?   Yes ___   No ___
5. Do you like to read cookbooks?   Yes ___   No ___
6. Do you like to read encyclopedias?   Yes ___   No ___
7. Do you ever use a dictionary?"   Yes ___   No ___
8. Do you think the school library media center has books that you want to read?   Yes ___   No ___
9. Do you like to read paperback books?   Yes ___   No ___
10. Do you like to read science fiction books?   Yes ___   No ___
11. Do you like to read books that give you information?   Yes ___   No ___
12. Do you like to read books that have a happy ending?   Yes ___   No ___
13. Have you ever bought a book on your own?   Yes ___   No ___
14. Do you take books along when you go on trips?   Yes ___   No ___
15. Do you think reading is important?   Yes ___   No ___
16. Do you watch television every day for at least 2 hours?   Yes ___   No ___
17. Did anyone read to you at home when you were younger?   Yes ___   No ___

18. Is someone reading to you now?   Yes ___   No ___
19. Do you ever read to someone in
    your family?   Yes ___   No ___
20. Have you ever given someone a
    book as a gift?   Yes ___   No ___

_____

Boy ___ Girl ___
Grade _____

Index

Alphabet books, use of with:
  first graders, 71–72
  infants, 6
  kindergarten children, 37
Amblyopia. *See* Lazy-eye blindness
Ann Landers' letters, 109–10
Audiovisual materials, use of:
  basal reader approach, 50–51
Auditory acuity:
  and reading readiness, 4
  infants, development of, 4–5
Auditory discrimination:
  infants, development of, 4–5

Basal reader approach:
  description of, 42–53
  pros and cons, 51–53
Basal reader lesson, 47–51
Basal readers:
  kindergarten children, 26–27
  selection of, 58–61
Bibliographies for:
  book bags, 69–70
  books about special problems and
    situations, 70
  parents, 19, 39–41
  reading readiness, 23–24, 39–40
Bibliographies, preparation of:
  for parents, 19–22, 39
  for special children, 22
Blume, Judy, 106
Book fairs, 19, 94
Books, how to select for and use
    with:
  disabled readers, 127–28

early readers, 74–75
first graders, 66–75
hearing impaired, 9–10
infants, 8–9
kindergarten children, 36–37
mentally handicapped, 11
second graders, 83–86
third through fifth graders, 106
visually impaired, 10
Bookstores:
  involvement in reading program,
    18–19, 94
Bruner, Jerome, 3
Bulletin boards, use of, 109

Card catalog, introduction of to:
  first graders, 57
  third graders, 106–7
Chall, Jean, 52
Children, special identification of:
  dyslexic, 125–26
  emotionally disabled, 10–11
  hearing impaired, 9–10
  mentally handicapped, 11
  minority, 11–12
  visually impaired, 10
Children's Choices program, 110–11
Clarke, Louise, 128
Comic books, use of, 102
Community resource file, 39
Comprehension skills, description of,
    44–45, 80–81
Computer-assisted instruction, 99–
    100
  for gifted students, 80